THE ORIGINS OF THE CHANCELLORSHIP
The Buried Report of 1948

UCLA campus on Charter Day, 1964.

THE ORIGINS OF THE CHANCELLORSHIP
The Buried Report of 1948

Eugene C. Lee

Foreword by Clark Kerr
Afterword by Charles E. Young

Chapters in the History of the
University of California
Number Three

Center for the Studies in Higher Education and
Institute of Governmental Studies
University of California, Berkeley
1995

Library of Congress Cataloging-In-Publication Data
Lee, Eugene C.
    The origins of the chancellorship : the buried report of 1948 / Eugene
C. Lee
    p. cm. — (Chapters in the history of the University of California ; no. 3)
    Includes bibliographical references
    ISBN 0-87772-360-5
    1. University of California, Berkeley—History. I. Title. II. Series.
LD758.L44 1994
378.974'67—dc20   94-24409
                                              CIP

*To Joanne and Frank and to the memory of
Edwin A. and Edna Canfield Lee.*

Figure 1: President Sproul singing "All Hail" at a University
meeting in 1947, just after he had refused a more lucrative position. The sign reads "Stick with us, Bob."

In honor of the 125th anniversary of the founding of the University of California, the Center for Studies in Higher Education at Berkeley, in cooperation with the Institute of Governmental Studies, takes pleasure in publishing a series of "chapters" in the history of the University. These are designed to illuminate particular problems and periods in the history of U.C., especially its oldest and original campus at Berkeley, and to identify special turning points or features in the "long century" of the University's evolution. Histories are stories meant to be read and enjoyed in their own right, but the editors cannot conceal the hope that readers of these chapters will notice facts and ideas pertinent to the decade that closes our own century and millennium.

Carroll Brentano and
Sheldon Rothblatt, editors

Figure 2: Provost Dykstra, President Sproul, and the author, 1946.

FOREWORD

Eugene C. Lee has written an illuminating, authoritative, and balanced account of the early years (1944-1952) of what turned out to be a more than 20-year reorganization process (1943-1966) of the University of California. That reorganization has been the major one in the entire past history of the University and prospectively will remain so throughout the now foreseeable future history. It took the university from an approach that might be identified as "one campus with several locations" to "several campuses with coordinated policies and budgets."

The "one campus" approach was that of Robert Gordon Sproul who advanced it and defended it and administered it effectively during his 28 years as president (1930-1958). He was convinced that this was the only way to hold the University together. Lee concludes by saying that "only with chancellors actually in place [1952] would this belief [in 'centralized administration'] be challenged." It was challenged, but mostly withstood the challenges during the duration of Sproul's term of office to 1958. It was only thereafter that the University really moved to decentralized administration. For example, by 1966, 99 percent of academic personnel decisions were decided at the campus level. The skirmishes, in the meantime (1952-1958), were difficult for both sides. In the end, decentralization was achieved *and* the University was held together with less resistance than under the "one campus" approach that was in the process of disintegration in the course of growth in numbers of campuses and of students and faculty members—useful as it had once been.

Lee is the one person in the best position to review this important aspect of the history of the University of California. He was an undergraduate at UCLA from 1943 to 1946 (and president of the student body and member of the football team) as that campus began to mature as a research university and to demand its "place in the sun." He served as an assistant to the survey of the University's administration by the Public Administration Service in 1948. Subsequently, he was a long-time faculty member in the political science department at Berkeley and, from 1967 to 1988, director of the Institute of Governmental Studies. While a faculty member, he served as a faculty assistant to the chancellor at Berkeley during the early battles over decentralization, and later as a vice-president of the University with responsibility for the final stages of the monumental decentralization that took place from 1958 to 1966. He has continued to be consulted on University organizational matters by each of the five presidents from 1966 to 1993.

Lee thus writes both from a careful review of the formal record and a hands-on experience with the informal intensity of the debates. A new structure for the University was being created, and it became a model that other universities came to study—it has several times been cited as the most successful of all such systems. That was a time when "systems" were being established or reexamined all over the nation, and Lee and his colleague Frank Bowen later made the definitive study of them for the Carnegie Commission on Higher Education.* Lee also has consulted widely on the governance of university systems both in the United States and abroad, including the University of London, which is the oldest and most famous of such systems.

I am greatly indebted to Gene Lee, for he was my "point man" on decentralization at crucial times both when I was chancellor at Berkeley and later president of

---

*Eugene C. Lee and Frank M. Bowen, *The Multicampus University: A Study of Academic Governance* (New York: McGraw-Hill, 1971).

the University of California. He had the expertise, the patience, and the personality to help work through what sometimes seemed in advance to be problems impossible of easy solutions, but he made them look easy. Few people have both written so well about the history of the University of California and served that history so well.

Clark Kerr
President Emeritus

ACKNOWLEDGEMENTS

This account of a major development in the administrative history of the University of California draws almost entirely on four major sources. The author owes a special debt of gratitude to University Archivist William M. Roberts of the Bancroft Library; Anne L. Shaw, Assistant Secretary of the Board of Regents; Willa Baum, Head of the Regional Oral History Office at Berkeley; and Dale E. Treleven and David S. Zeidberg of the Oral History Program at UCLA. In addition, the author has benefited greatly from the comments of many reviewers, who kindly consented to read earlier drafts of the monograph.

Special thanks, too, to Sheldon Rothblatt and to Clark Kerr and Charles Young (first chancellor and longest-serving chancellor, respectively) for sharing their comments—providing a broadly informed context for the study.

The entire project would not have been possible without the leadership and assistance of Carroll Brentano, Project Coordinator of the University History Project. The monograph was ably produced by Kimberly Patton of the Political Science Department and Maria Wolf of the Institute of Governmental Studies.

ILLUSTRATIONS

All illustrations except the cover and frontispiece (courtesy of the UCLA Archives) and Figures 2 and 7 (property of the author), are courtesy of the Bancroft Library.

INTRODUCTION

In the following chapter, Professor Eugene C. Lee examines the origins of the "chancellorial" system of the University of California, an organizational structure composed of nine apparently autonomous campuses linked to a central office now in Oakland under the leadership of a "president." Until the creation of the multicampus system, a process starting in the 1930s, the University of California was virtually the single campus of Berkeley from which the president administered a "southern branch" in Los Angeles, an agricultural program at Davis, a medical school in San Francisco, and technical and extension programs. Lee tells the story of the University's expansion largely from the "inside," relying heavily upon the correspondence of leading personalities, especially the indefatigable and strong-minded president, Robert Gordon Sproul. Lee's account brings an immediacy to the story. The creation of today's University of California was hardly a straightforward affair, an inevitable development bound to occur no matter who were leaders and actors. On the contrary, as there are many different types of multicampus systems in the United States today, with different missions, different styles of governance, and different kinds of boards of trustees, so could the University of California have assumed a different form. Lee provides a first step in trying to explain how it assumed the form it still essentially possesses.

The undertaking is important. A multicampus system is an odd creation, not exactly in keeping with historical precedents. It requires a close look. But before we can even begin to describe the university of "licensed branches," we have to consider how to define the institution commonly called a "university." So popular is the word in

America that it is safe to assume that most students and their families, or even most professors, do not realize how vexed and troublesome the word has been. Innumerable and contradictory definitions exist, if for no other reason than the hoary fact that universities themselves have existed for more than 700 years. Over such a span of time, no institution ever remains quite the same, no matter how steady it seems to appear. Curricula, affiliated schools and colleges, the composition of boards of trustees, internal administration, examination systems, course structures, the relations that universities have with society and with governments differ greatly from country to country and within the same country.

Most American alumni and certainly most undergraduates provide a relatively easy answer to the question of defining a university. A university is simply a fixed "place," a geographical location most often consisting of a blend of gardens and buildings, walks and recreational facilities. One goes to a "place" as one goes to work or to the beach.

In any common meaning of the word, it is clearly impossible to "attend" a multicampus system of more than one place. Our "loyal" alumni can only be loyal to a campus. The same is true for faculty, students and staff. The dominant symbols of university life are specific to the campus, not to the "legal" university. Graduation ceremonies tie the departing students to the campus not to the system. The chancellor not the president represents the university to its interior publics. And so our normal comprehension of a university as a single location is understandably the prevailing and favored view.

Yet quietly, now almost unintrusively, the larger presence of the "presidential" University of California critically determines the overall financial and political health of the system, guiding its manifold relationships with the most populated of all American states and one whose wealth and idiosyncratic political and social cultures make California into virtually a distinct nation.

The multicampus, "federal" or "federated" (even "confederated") university is distinctly American in historical origin. To be sure, there were precedents of sorts in the "second" University of London founded in 1836, but this type of English university, to include successors coming later in the nineteenth century, was designed expressly to guarantee a high national degree standard. It did not really serve as a model for America. New English provincial and regional universities were to be prevented from offering curricula and teaching deemed to be inconsistent with past national practice, especially as represented by Oxford and Cambridge universities. Once new universities had successfully internalized the proper standards, they could be "dismissed" from the system and permitted single-campus independence outside the national capital. The London example was followed in the University of Wales, which still exists as a federation of university colleges, and to some extent in Ireland.

The University of London was not only the center of a national system of new institutions. It was also an imperial university. University colleges established in the vast reaches of the British Empire, in Canada, Africa, India, Australia, and New Zealand, were outposts of the headquarters in London. Students in those lands studied for an "external degree," and when the twentieth century began the granting of external degrees was as important a function of the University of London as the award of "internal" degrees.

In time regional colleges, and imperial university colleges, achieved separation. The University of London remains in theory, and to some extent in practice, a multicampus university, but the campuses are as much specialized schools and colleges as they are wholly separate universities. The practice of creating multicampus systems is far more prevalent in today's United States than in Britain, especially the practice of creating more than one multicampus system within each state, and on the European Continent it is a distinctly rare undertaking, the greatly centralized French higher education system notwithstanding.

The American multicampus university is therefore a fascinating historical phenomenon. Its distinctiveness calls out for explanation. One answer is that a federal university, however unusual in the history of universities as such, makes perfect sense in an American context. The American constitution is decentralized. It is natural for Americans to think of expansion as a combination of local and central factors. The nation grew in such fashion, as new continental territories with their embryonic governments applied to Washington for the benefits that membership in the whole would provide. The history of public universities is consequently parallel.

This answer is broadly helpful if not sufficiently detailed. As the story being told here very clearly explains, there is a difference between the fact of a solar system of campuses and the way in which the distant circling planets respect the heliocentric authority. The organization of a federated university can never be a settled matter. The multicampus system produces a continual tug-of-war between the presidential center and the chancellorial periphery. That conflict is sometimes the result of the play of personalities locked into disagreement and sometimes the result of larger influences having to do with population, regional interests, and politics.

For most of its history since its founding over 125 years ago, the University of California was synonymous with Berkeley. The campus was located reasonably close to the state capital in Sacramento, and the north-central portion of the state dominated the south. But as the valleys and coastal areas of Los Angeles filled in and expanded in economic and political influence, the demand for higher education in the south similarly increased, placing formidable pressure on a University of California leadership located on the Berkeley campus. The pressure became even greater after 1945. California recovered from a war economy, and demographic growth was irresistible, as it appears to be today in the 1990s. It would be impossible to accommodate an indefinite number of students on a single campus, if for no other basic reason than residential education was too expensive for most Americans.

President Sproul, in a memorable Jane Austen paraphrase that Lee has uncovered, did not like "local prides and prejudices." He represented the "great tradition" of Anglo-American university building in this sense, that a rapid expansion in numbers leading to the creation of geographically separate campuses threatened the unity of the University as he knew it, its sense of place, its pleasing symbolism, its support network of alumni, and its ability to set academic standards. Indeed, the federal University of California has been able to maintain a considerable central identity over the past 30 or more years. A single Academic Senate, similar, perhaps identical, stated degree and admission requirements, a common salary schedule are conspicuous features.

Personality factors are certainly not absent from the story. Quite obviously Sproul preferred being wholly in command. Nevertheless, his primary concern, as Lee notes, was a fear that a divided university would provide greater opportunities for legislative competition and intervention. Subsequent presidents have certainly shared Sproul's fear.

However much President Sproul attempted to deflect pressures and recommendations for a system of full or partially independent campuses—Lee shows how he almost suppressed the Public Administration Service Report of 1948—a multicampus system of some kind was in the offing. The interesting questions therefore are related to the specific kind of overall governing organization required of a system, probably, one might add, any system. What should be the exact degree of local versus central authority, the kinds of reporting lines to be created and the powers of chancellors (even their titles) relative to that of the president? Should a chief campus officer (to use today's corporate-induced terminology) report directly to the president, or to an assistant? Should he or she report directly to the regents, going around the president? Should some campus officers be allowed to bypass chancellors and report directly to the center? Should chancellorial authority extend to all programs on a campus, or only to the programs conventionally designated liberal arts, reserving such politically important areas as public health and agriculture for the president? Lee's account provides an unusually rich source of information on these issues, showing how many of them needed to be addressed. The problem of admissions also required attention. Should admissions be centralized, especially as admissions policy has always been a ticklish business in California, as in America generally, given populist traditions and mass markets. In such circumstances, meritocratic selection policies have generally been difficult to establish and uphold.

Other important dimensions of the governance process required attention, the role of the board of regents for example. Since the inception of the University of California, regents and presidents had both tussled and cooperated. Individual regents sometimes managed to exert considerable personal influence over the direction of university policy, or were even able to intervene in everyday operations. Indeed, the distinction between policy and operating details was never a clear one. It too was an area of University life where both personal styles and circumstances could vary, and did.

Historians like to identify turning points in history, the moment when a new direction occurs, when old habits die and new attitudes arise, or, to use a more sociological and philosophical vocabulary, when a "paradigm shift" occurs. This is the moment in history when the old ways are obsolete or superseded. The matrix of understanding has changed so much that inherited views are no longer tenable. To remain with the old manner is to hang quite out of fashion, like—to continue using Shakespeare's simile for the decline of feudalism—a rusty mail [i.e., suit of armor] in monumental mockery.

Sproul would have preferred authority concentrated in one place. This would make the task of "accountability" less difficult. It would provide for program, degree, and admissions quality and allow the University of California to maintain its identification with the renowned research universities of the world. "Local prides and prejudices" worked against the more "universal" aspects of a university, its cosmopolitan nature, its international reputation, its conformity to accepted criteria of excellence in scholarship and science.

But no matter how much Sproul regretted "local prides and prejudices," a paradigm shift was occurring. Demands for relevance and short-term goals could hardly be resisted. The California regions had greatly grown in economic strength. Their regional interests were better represented in the legislature, and their populations had become more varied, better able to express preferences and tastes. Also, over time the branches had produced their own loyal alumni, their own natural support bases that knew not Berkeley or what Berkeley had wrought.

A multicampus university, even one which in Sproul's words might be "a loosely knit federation of institutions without strong leadership," was in the offing. A rudimentary organization already existed. Furthermore, the differentiation and complexity so characteristic of all institutions, especially those like universities that pursue knowledge and "discovery," constituted a centrifugal force. A culture of disciplines and subdisciplines supports decentralized decision making as an intellectual necessity that leads to the growth of knowledge upon which current conceptions of personal and material well-being rest. Such a culture cannot be adjusted or controlled from the center without damaging the vitality of the academic periphery or dampening initiative.* High-tech industries today have arrived at a similar understanding and organization. Already Sproul's center was unable to respond to the needs of the "branches." Delays, hesitations, and overloads were becoming intolerable drawbacks.

Yet the question remains, why a multibranch, why a plural campus system? Why couldn't the University of California follow in the footsteps, so to speak, of the University of London and the similar federations established later in other parts of Britain? Once having sponsored and controlled regional campuses in England, university centers like London allowed them to separate, to become single-campus universities in their own right, with their own admissions and degree standards and powers of faculty recruitment and student selection. In retrospect, it seems sensible to believe that UCLA, for example, would certainly have desired full autonomy, being able to draw so successfully upon the vast resources of an enormous economy.

The answer is worth pondering and cannot be answered in this place. But one suggestion is possible. Perhaps UCLA and the other institutions of the 1950s, as well as those to be born in the 1960s, had more to gain from being attached to a center, particularly a center whose powers were in flux, evolving and uncertain, changing and capable of changing yet again, and therefore less of a threat to local prides and prejudices than at first assumed. That center, by its long association with Berkeley, also had the necessary international standing to make affiliation and name-sharing useful. Perhaps too—and this seems very likely—the leaders, scientists, and scholars of

---

*For an important discussion of these considerations, see Burton R. Clark, "The Problem of Complexity in Modern Higher Education," in *The European and American University since 1800: Historical and Sociological Essays*, ed. Sheldon Rothblatt and Björn Wittrock (Cambridge: Cambridge University Press, 1993), Chapter 7.

the branches and new campuses understood Sproul's point about the value of a unified system in a state where the political process so often appeared fickle and unpredictable and where a common effort would reduce the vulnerability of satellite campuses.

Perhaps too our search for an answer should take us outside the University of California and its branches, field laboratories, programs, and campuses to note what other features of an energetic Pacific Coast state might have been influential.

Competition, it has been noted, drives American higher education towards excellence, or towards markets, or towards specific programs and study arrangements. The University of California was not the only publicly supported higher education system in the state. State colleges (now the California State University System) were plentiful, active, and growing, eager to share in the educational resources that a rich and variegated economy was making available. Before 1960, the boundaries between the missions of the state colleges and the University of California were not yet fixed in a Master Plan for Higher Education. Mission duplication, lobbying in Sacramento, the scramble for money and students were the likely scenarios—indeed, the reality.** This was a reality that the University of London, part of a culture where universities were not expected to compete with one another, did not have to face.

**President Emeritus Clark Kerr addresses similar questions in a fascinating autobiographical essay on the Master Plan. See his "The California Master Plan of 1960 for Higher Education: An *Ex Ante* View, in *The OECD, the Master Plan and the California Dream: a Berkeley Conversation*, ed. Sheldon Rothblatt (Berkeley: Center for Studies in Higher Education, 1992), Chapter 3. Reprinted in Clark Kerr, *Higher Education Cannot Escape History* (Albany: State University of New York Press, 1994), Chapter 8.

Lacking this "protection," the University of California re-made itself into the special kind of university so evident today.

Sheldon Rothblatt

Figure 3: The Public Administration Report of 1948.

prejudices."* Concern over the potential divisiveness of such pressures, which dominated the president's thinking throughout his career, was more persuasive than the contrary position that "The task of administering a university with its two major centers five hundred miles apart may be beyond the capacity of any man to do well."[12] However, this latter theme was to be forcefully raised only five years later.

PRESSURES FOR CHANGE

Pressures for administrative change arose in part, suggests Stadtman, out of faculty restiveness over conditions imposed by World War II, coupled with the retirement in 1942 of Earle Hedrick, UCLA's vice-president and provost.[13] Advising the Board of Regents that it would be especially difficult to recruit a successor during the wartime emergency, Sproul's solution was to place the campus under the direction of a three-man "interim administrative committee" and to postpone filling the UCLA vacancy "on the understanding that he would give a major part of his time to Los Angeles. . . . [T]he work of the University [Sproul told the Regents] could probably be handled satisfactorily under this system, since the routines are well crystallized at Berkeley, with its longer history, and do not demand as much of the President's personal time."[14]

---

*Stadtman describes the character of the centralized administration:

> In practice, the power enjoyed by Deutsch and Moore [the provosts of Berkeley and Los Angeles] on their respective campuses was limited. Sproul retained authority in all budget matters and in the appointment of tenure faculty members, department chairmen, and deans. Neither could easily contravene the directives of the comptroller on business matters affecting their campuses.[11]

Figure 4: Monroe E. Deutsch dedicating the Wheeler bust, 1928.

Figure 5: Joel H. Hilldebrand, 1946.

This emphasis on the special needs of UCLA, over-shadowing those at Berkeley, was to be repeated many times in the years ahead. The message was not lost on the older campus. Dean Joel Hildebrand, one of Sproul's key supporters, characterized faculty sentiment in a speech to the Berkeley Academic Senate in 1943:

. . . the President divides his attention between seven campuses[15] and numerous public affairs. There is little delegation of authority, even when the President is absent. The government is then carried on by mail. There is no administrative officer whose business it is to sit down and discuss with a department chairman the work, welfare, and future of his department.

Our basic need is a change in the form and function of the university administration to provide for delegation of authority to persons who can gain and hold the confidence both of the President and of the members of the faculty with whom they deal.[16]

At the same meeting of the Academic Senate, a "committee on the organization of the university" was established, an action that was paralleled in Los Angeles by the Senate's southern section.

Sproul's reaction to Hildebrand's remarks, contained in a letter to the chair of the new committee at Berkeley, was immediate:

. . . no one knows better than I that the present University organization is not well fitted to the needs of today. . . . [It] fails mainly in that it places upon the President the impossible task of coordinating and leading literally hundreds of administrators and not a few faculty members, while at the same time discharging public and semipublic functions which would fill all the time of most men . . . the fundamental need is for more and better administrators . . . the number of key persons dealing with the President must be reduced . . . there will be no objection on the part of the President, but rather the reverse, to further delegation of authority to administrative officers chosen by him under a new plan of organization.[17]

In a separate internal memorandum, the president stated his belief in "centralization of policy making in the office of the chief administrator (the President), with a corresponding decentralization of execution at regional, divisional, and departmental levels . . . delegation of authority and responsibility for execution should be granted as close to the actual carrying out of the task as possible."[18]

Sproul's new plan was not, however, a strengthened campus executive with delegated authority. Instead, he proposed that the entire University be organized along divisional lines similar to the pattern of agriculture. Engineering, humanities, medical sciences, natural sciences, and social sciences would be organized under administrators with direct authority for departments related to their division on all campuses.

> It is my belief based upon wide experience, that a plan of organization along these lines indicated would have possibilities of numerous advantages, under proper direction, in facilitating suitable development of departmental programs, in promoting coordination of effort and cooperation in attacking common problems, in providing a readier means of access to responsible administrative authority, and in providing department chairmen with an opportunity [as suggested by Joel Hildebrand] "to sit down and discuss . . . the work, welfare and future" of their departments.[19]*

---

*Robert S. Johnson, a special assistant to President Sproul, commented on this proposal, which the president continued to consider and subsequently proposed to the Public Administration Service team:

8

Such an administrative structure, centralized albeit dispersed, was not what the two faculty committees on university organization envisaged. Instead, they recommended:

> . . . a general administrative officer (provost or other designation) should be located at each of the two general university centers (Berkeley and Los Angeles), empowered to exercise general administrative functions over that center and associated campuses at all times. . . . The number of individual cases to be decided by the President personally, and the number of documents requiring the President's personal signature, should be held to a minimum—only the most important and serious cases should come under his personal scrutiny. . . .
> The committees expect to make more specific suggestions along these lines. . . .[21]

The informal comment of a faculty member was even more candid. After complaining that the president's secretary and administrative assistant were exercising too much influence, the note concludes:

> The multiplication of so-called "All-University" officers should cease. It is far better to concentrate responsibility on each campus. . . . The Pres-

---

Because as a member of his staff I had been assigned to the survey team by the president, I felt called upon to defend the Sproul proposal as best I could, but I got nowhere. . . . [T]he campus heads would have been no more than coordinators attempting vainly to mediate between the competing claims of the various faculties for facilities and services. Student loyalties, particularly under-graduate loyalties, are attached more to campuses than to academic disciplines. Other insuperable difficulties were also pointed out, and I had to concede to the others [on] the survey team that the president's scheme would not work. I'm sure that he, too, came readily to agree.[20]

Figure 6: Regent Dickson, Sproul, and Provost Emeritus E. C. Moore, UCLA, 1944.

ident should not struggle—or have to struggle—with details.[22]

The concerns of the faculty in this period do not appear to have engendered much discussion among the regents. In contrast, the views of UCLA alumni did attract their attention. In May 1943, the Blue Shield, a group of alumni leaders, presented to the regents a resolution that a full-time executive be immediately appointed for the campus, that "he have full authority in matters exclusively affecting the University of California at Los Angeles. . . . That this position be given a title having the prestige that such a man and position deserve, and that this title preferably be President or Chancellor" and that the regents themselves undertake the search and make the appointment for the UCLA executive.[23] Without further comment and without any visible communication with northern colleagues, Blue Shield also suggested that a similar title be given the head of the Berkeley campus.

In a subsequent memorandum, apparently following consultation with Blue Shield and reflecting the views of the Academic Senate's southern committee on organization, Regent Dickson of Los Angeles presented a proposal calling for the appointment of a provost, on nomination of the president, with "general powers over the affairs of the Southern Section of the University," including the appointment of department chairmen and supervision of the local business office. The two provosts (north and south) would be invited to sit as "observers" at meetings of the regents.[24]

At the ensuing regents' meeting in October 1943, the president proposed and the board approved the appointment of a provost with

> full authority, under the President, to administer the departments on the Los Angeles and La Jolla campuses. . . . [T]he decisions of the Provost in matters affecting these departments will be final if he acts in accordance with the policies laid down

by the Board of Regents and the President and
within the limits of the annual budgets established
by the Board.

The intent of these changes, the president repeated, was
to centralize policymaking in the office of the president
and to decentralize the execution of policies.[25]

In his letter to Clarence Dykstra, president of the
University of Wisconsin, inviting him to accept the
provostship at UCLA, President Sproul spelled out the
difference between the two university systems: "[Y]ou
would deal with, report to, and be responsible to the
President of the University rather than its Board of
Regents. . . . The Provost is the responsible executive, *de
facto*, not *de jure*, for a campus. . . . The authority of the
Provost is authority delegated to him by the President and
is complete within the delegation."[26] Left unstated was
the extent of the delegation and the reality of "*de jure*"
executive authority. Provost Dykstra would quickly
discover that Westwood was not Madison.

The authority of the campus executive, with respect
both to Los Angeles *and* to Berkeley, became a central
theme, albeit implicit, in the reports of the Academic
Senate's southern and northern committees on organization. For example, the southern committee concluded that
"By delegation from the President, the Provost should
exercise a considerable portion of the duties, powers, and
responsibilities vested in the President by the Regents . . .
[including] general supervision over the local business
office."[27] The northern committee, perhaps more experienced and more bold, was less guarded in its comments:

[T]he President undertakes to handle too many
administrative functions, so that material inroads
are made even on his remarkable supply of energy,
and his time for the more important presidential
functions is seriously curtailed. . . . [I]t would save
much time of the President and of many others if
certain types of cases were definitely understood to
lie normally within the Provost's sphere of action.[28]

The committee suggested that the provost's powers might include appointment of assistant professors, action on leaves of absence, and authority to transfer funds within departmental budgets.

These suggestions for specific delegations of authority were in marked contrast to the delay in obtaining formal statements concerning the existing powers of the two provosts. In early 1946, two years after Dykstra's arrival at UCLA, the chair of the Senate's southern committee on organization noted in a letter to President Sproul that it was "not aware that a notice setting forth the specific duties, powers and responsibilities you have delegated to Provost Dykstra has been issued. . . . The committee is aware of the existence on this campus of some degree of perplexity and uncertainty."[29]

The president's somewhat oblique response was to refer to a notice describing the authority of the newly appointed vice-president of the University, who was jointly dean of the College of Agriculture with delegated authority "to administer the activities of the University in the field of agriculture. . . . *Similar authority has been delegated to Vice-President Deutsch for the departments on the Berkeley campus, and to Provost Dykstra for those on the Los Angeles and La Jolla campuses.*[30] "It would seem to me," the president suggested to the UCLA committee chairman, "that this announcement meets the terms [of your letter]."[31]

One month later, the president had a change of heart and issued a formal announcement to department chairmen and other administrative officers:

My attention has been called to the fact that no announcement concerning the responsibilities laid upon the Provost of the University of California, resident upon the Los Angeles Campus, by the recent administrative reorganization of the University, has been made except indirectly. To correct this situation, this notice has been prepared and distributed. Provost Dykstra has full authority,

Figure 7: Provost and Mrs. Dykstra and President and Mrs. Sproul, c. 1946.

delegated to him by the President of the University, to administer all departments on the Los Angeles and La Jolla campuses, with the exception of those departments such as Agriculture and Public Health, for which there are special organizational arrangements. The statewide departments, such as the Personnel Office, the Accounting Office, the Business Office, the Office of Relations with Schools, the Office of the Director of Admissions, the Office of Public Information, the Bureau of Guidance and Placement, the Division of Vocational Education, the University Press, and University Extension, are not, of course, included within the authority of the Provost but are administered by the President directly.

In accordance with the Standing Orders of the Regents, the President appoints chairmen of departments, but all business of the departments goes through the Office of the Provost, and his decisions, made in accordance with the policies laid down by the Regents and the President of the University, are final if financial requirements are within the limits of the annual budget established by the Regents. . . .[32]

In November, the president issued an almost identical statement concerning the Berkeley campus:

Vice-President Deutsch has called my attention to the fact that no announcement concerning the responsibilities laid upon him by the administrative reorganization of the University has been made, other than indirectly. Therefore, this statement is published.[33]

The announcement stated that the vice-president had "full authority delegated to him by the President of the University to administer all departments on the Berkeley campus" but, as in the Los Angeles memorandum, listed the exceptions of such departments as agriculture, nursing and physiology, "for which there are special organizational arrangements" and the "statewide departments"—personnel, accounting and business offices—which were "administered by the President directly." The statement concluded, as had the Los Angeles announcement, with the now familiar theme that the purpose of this pattern of organization was "to centralize policy-making in the office of the President and to decentralize the execution of policies."

It would take 20 years for this general principle to be implemented in a form similar to today's multicampus university. But in 1946 the balance was different. For President Sproul, the unity of the university was paramount. Robert S. Johnson, a senior staff associate in the president's office, comments: "[President] Sproul not only relished the exercise of power, but he was also fearful that too much decentralization of power would end in disintegration of the university. Sproul was determined to defend the integrity of the University of California, a single institution located on several campuses under a single chief executive reporting to a single governing board."[34] The "administrative reorganization" referred to in the Dykstra and Deutsch announcements amounted to modest clarification of authority but no fundamental change. Offered the presidency of Columbia, the president sought the advice of the regents. Did the board, Sproul asked, "still adhere to the policy of a statewide university with one board, one president, and a centralized organization such as now exists?" The regents responded: "[T]he unity of the University shall be considered sacred. . . . The Regents all concur in the efforts made by the President to maintain the integrity and oneness of the University's system."[35]

THE PUBLIC ADMINISTRATION SERVICE SURVEY

Given his vote of confidence by the regents, his decision to continue as president and his reluctance to increase significantly the delegated authority of the campus provosts, it is not clear just what motivated President Sproul to recommend an administrative survey of the University. Neither the minutes of the Board of Regents nor the president's own files provide a basis for judgment. One may speculate, on the basis of his comments noted below, that his concern was the organization of the systemwide administration, rather than the distribution of authority between the central office and the campuses. He may also have been influenced by the retirement of Monroe Deutsch in August 1947, leaving the Berkeley campus under the direct administration of the president. Unquestionably, too, the president felt the impact of the recent inclusion within the University system of the Santa Barbara campus, and the legislature's appropriation of $2,000,000 in 1948 for a study of four-year liberal arts colleges at Riverside and Davis. In a letter to a statewide committee requesting that it study expansion of university facilities, the president observed that "whatever recommendations seem wise to the Committee concerning Riverside will have effect on, and application to, similar expansion at Davis."[36]

Whatever the rationale, the first reference to the desirability of an outside administrative study appears in the report of a UCLA "committee on simplification of university procedure," appointed by the president in February 1946 and chaired by the dean of education, Edwin A. Lee. The committee recommended that "the President consider most carefully the advisability of having an adequate study of University procedure made by an outside group of competence and standing. Such a group would approach the task objectively and dispassionately, and having no other responsibility, could give full time and attention to the study. . . . [Y]our Committee can think of no better investment of funds in terms of real return to the University."[37]

In October 1947, Public Administration Service (PAS), a nonprofit consulting firm serving public agencies, was invited to submit a proposal. They recently had completed surveys of the universities of Purdue, Minnesota, and Puerto Rico and had been recommended by two of President Sproul's key associates:

We are both convinced that someone from outside looking at our statewide University organization can contribute a great deal to improvement of our administrative procedures and organization. Too often in the past few years members of our administrative staff have collapsed because of pressure of work and either the volume is too great or the red tape too cumbersome or the personnel too limited to do the work of this fast-growing University properly.[38]

President Sproul replied:

While I cannot accept the reasons stated in your memorandum of October 9, believing them to be generalizations drawn from an inadequate sampling, I am in hearty accord with your proposal that the Public Administration Service (PAS) be employed to make a survey of the general administrative organization of the University, and I shall so recommend to the Regents at the October meeting.[39]

The president's recommendation, he informed the regents, was "based on the fact that the great growth of the University, the increase in enrollment and addition of campuses and stations during the war and post-war period has made such a review of existing administrative organization and practices desirable, and the continuing pressure of business is such that it cannot be halted to permit chief administrative officers to effectively survey their organization and operations." Regent Dickson expressed the hope that the regents be consulted from time to time and "help guide [the survey team] in the formulation of its report. He gave as his example his interest in having the consultants consider "a possible change in the administration of the University of California at Los Angeles from a provost system to a committee system" (a plan that, as noted below, he continued to advocate as late as 1950). Regent Neylan disagreed:

> [I]f it is understood that the group is to make a searching investigation, [I] would rather not complicate their general assignment by either qualifying it or amending it by implication or otherwise. . . . A prior meeting with The Regents would destroy the value of an independent view and independent judgment.

After further discussion, it was recommended to the board that PAS be employed at a cost not to exceed $20,000.[40]

The survey team began its work in January 1948, led by John Blandford, an experienced public executive who had served as assistant director of the U.S. Bureau of the Budget and federal housing administrator in the Roosevelt administration. The methodology of the study followed standard consulting procedures—a thorough review of documentary materials and interviews with more than two hundred faculty members and administrators at campus and statewide levels. Along with administrative organization charts, reports, and other descriptive materials, written suggestions were solicited concerning changes in organizational structure or administrative practices deemed desirable.

Two such responses are particularly significant. Provost Dykstra, whose distinguished career included city management and direction of the national selective service system, as well as the Wisconsin presidency, commented:

> The problem of decentralization in administration needs thorough study. I believe the president thinks we have decentralized pretty completely, but old ways and old habits throughout the organization tend to neutralize the directives which have been given. As an illustration, the directives setting up the provost office indicate that he is in administrative charge on a given campus. Practically this is not true as will be seen by reference

to the chart of the provost's office. Moreover, the vertical lines of authority that run from top to bottom [for example, from the campus business manager to the comptroller] have few cross-over or horizontal lines. This fact leaves the provost in the dark in many matters on his own campus and all the while it is assumed that he knows. . . .

[I]t is an interesting fact, for instance, that the local business office is represented at Regents' meetings, the architect's office is represented as is the public information office, but the provost is not and does not even find out except through the press what the Regents have done.

In my opinion, the president should have a much larger freedom of action than the Regents now allow. Most actions of the president should be reported to the Regents as something done. . . . The fact that many matters must be presented to the Regents cause administrative delays running up to thirty days or more.

I have continued to believe in one university for the state. The agitation for more than one or for what is called separation is kept alive, so far as this campus is concerned, by what we might call frustration of faculty and administrative officers. Delay, review, inaction, inability to get answers to questions and letters, powers exercised by the central business office, "coordination" of things not easily brought together, all of these things among others feed the flames of "separation."[41]

Dykstra's handwritten note on a copy of the memorandum that he sent to President Sproul for his information is indicative of the climate surrounding the survey: "Pres. Sproul: In connection with the report of P.A.S., you may wish to have this statement which no one but you knows about. You will recall that you thought that this should not get into the files. C.A.D." The frustration of Clarence Dykstra was also felt by his counter-part at Berkeley, as

Dean Emeritus Sanford Elberg recounts: "Monroe Deutsch, once in an unguarded moment, shared with me his disappointment over the lack of Vice-Presidential and Provostial authority."[42]

A detailed response to the survey team's request came from the Academic Senate advisory committee to the president following its discussions with PAS staff. The 15-page memorandum, representing both Berkeley and Los Angeles views, was probably close to a faculty consensus, at least as far as a leadership position could be defined. The committee called for a "delegation of authority on a large scale [and the] organization of most university activities upon a regional rather than upon a functional basis . . . [which would] give to local faculties a large sense of participation in the conduct of their own part of the university, fostering their interest and loyalty." (Agriculture and University Extension, the committee concluded, might continue to be administered on a statewide functional basis.) The resulting organizational structure, the committee stated, should give the local campus administrator as much autonomy as possible consistent with broad general policies of the regents and the president. The campus administrative and academic head—the provost—should have the authority to prepare and administer the campus budget, to decide on all academic appointments and promotions, to appoint department chairmen and to "coordinate" and "integrate" the campus representatives of statewide business offices, such as accounting and buildings and grounds.[43]

President Sproul's suggestions to the survey team, at least as revealed in the files, were of a different character and focused on the staffing and organization of the central administration. "As a result of conferences in the East, I should like to emphasize the following items for consideration by your group because the procedures of certain other institutions seem to be superior to those of U.C., and the trend seems to be definitely in the directions indicated."[44] The record does not reveal what "other

Figure 8: James Corley and Baldwin Woods, c. 1955.

Figure 9: Edwin A. Lee, Dean of Education (UCLA).

institutions" the president had in mind, but he raised as issues of particular interest the administration of medical activities, perhaps at a vice-presidential level; the administration of organized research activities, perhaps under a director of organized research; and the "device of a bureau of the budget."

For his part, Comptroller James Corley suggested consideration "of establishing on the Los Angeles campus a statewide office representing the President and/or the Comptroller at least, and possibly some of the other statewide officers. . . . Decisions are often delayed because of the absence of a statewide officer on our Los Angeles campus."[45] That delays could be reduced by delegating greater authority to campus officials, more specifically the provost, was not suggested. Robert Rogers, a financial administrator at UCLA for nearly 40 years, provides an insight into the relationships that existed between the outlying campuses and the central administration:

> Taylor [UCLA business manager], Corley [University comptroller], Underhill [secretary-treasurer of the Regents], Sproul, all of those were UC Berkeley graduates. They could not recognize the inevitability that UCLA would rise and become a real rival of Berkeley and, in some ways, exceed Berkeley. And you must remember, in those days there was no universitywide administration. *The Berkeley campus administration was the coordinating one.*[46]

In short, not only the distance between campus and central administration fueled Los Angeles' concerns, but the fact that the central administration was so closely linked to that of the main and rival campus. George Pettit, one of President Sproul's closest associates, put the issue succinctly: "Berkeley's trouble is that it refuses to recognize that its daughter [UCLA] has become a sister."[47]

The above contrasting views provide the context within which the survey team operated. On the one hand, the campuses—faculty and administrators alike—called for a decentralization of authority from the regents to the president and thence to the provost. The president and comptroller, in contrast, focused their attention on the structure of the central administration. These two themes, authority and structure, were to dominate the debate over University organization for many years. In 1948, they became the concern of the PAS survey team.

THE REPORT

The report, delivered to the president in mid-1948, stressed *both* structure and authority, but clearly its most provocative recommendations called for a sweeping delegation of decision making to the campuses. For this to be done, however, the regents would first have to change radically their historic mode of behavior. Perhaps because of sensitivity over this issue, as well as conflicting advice from campus and universitywide officials, to be discussed below, the president delayed release of the report to the board until March 1949.

The report itself opened with a brief summary of the history of the University of California, stressing the development of a statewide university system, the evolution of its organization and the timeliness of the survey:

A strategic moment has been chosen for inspecting and strengthening the University administrative structure. This structure has been heavily loaded and strained to capacity by its war and postwar services and obligations. Consequently, this is a period when strength is demonstrated and weakness is revealed—a profitable period for observation and for constructive proposal.[48]

The purpose of the survey, the report indicated, was to "identify current problems and seek constructive answers which would ease the road ahead. . . . [I]n the interest of time and space, the emphasis of the report is on deficiencies and on their correction."[49] No mention in the report was made of the University's responsibilities for the

Berkeley Radiation Laboratory or Los Alamos, these having been apparently excluded from the survey team's mandate.

The heart of the report was contained in two chapters: "Appraisal of the Administrative Organization" and "Proposals as to Administrative Organization." The first moved in its description from the Board of Regents downward to the department chairman, while the second proceeded in reverse order, from the department upward. Thus, the regents had only to read to page 15 to see the thrust of the report's observations concerning their activities:

> [T]he Board of Regents is the point of departure for examining the University's administrative organization; the volume and nature of administrative traffic through its committees and Board meetings inevitably affect the entire University administrative structure.[50]

A review of the agenda and minutes of board meetings revealed the regents' concern with a large volume and variety of specific actions. The report concluded that the board "retains and exercises administrative control on management problems and makes the decisions on detailed and relatively minor matters as well as on those of major significance and importance."[51] In what must have been one of its least popular statements among many regents, the report concluded:

> In the light of [its distinguished] membership, it is suggested that much of the current business of the Board is not of sufficient stature to challenge the full potential of its contribution. The flood of detail as to appointments, contracts, and budget transfers encumbers the agenda, tends to submerge items of major policy, and burdens the President's office; such business underestimates or understates the role of the Board. . . . [T]his unprofitable use of the rich resources of Regent experience represents a generous offering of Re-

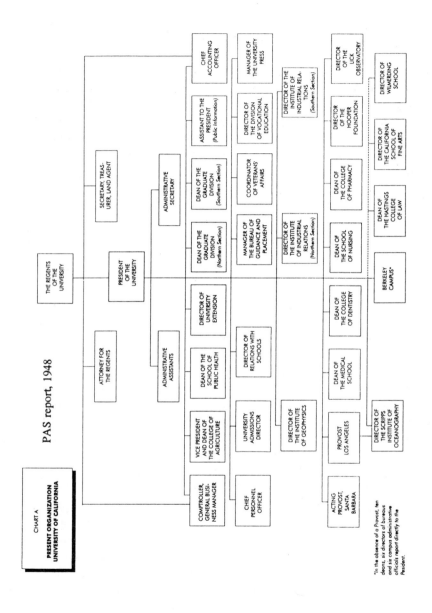

CHART A

**PRESENT ORGANIZATION
UNIVERSITY OF CALIFORNIA**

PAS report, 1948

In the absence of a Provost, ten deans, six directors of bureaus and six campus administrative officials report directly to the President.

THE REGENTS OF THE UNIVERSITY

PRESIDENT OF THE UNIVERSITY

SECRETARY, TREASURER, LAND AGENT

ATTORNEY FOR THE REGENTS

COMPTROLLER, GENERAL BUSINESS MANAGER

CHIEF PERSONNEL OFFICER

VICE PRESIDENT AND DEAN OF THE COLLEGE OF AGRICULTURE

UNIVERSITY ADMISSIONS DIRECTOR

DIRECTOR OF THE INSTITUTE OF GEOPHYSICS

ACTING PROVOST, SANTA BARBARA

PROVOST LOS ANGELES

DIRECTOR OF THE SCRIPPS INSTITUTE OF OCEANOGRAPHY

ADMINISTRATIVE ASSISTANTS

DEAN OF THE SCHOOL OF PUBLIC HEALTH

DIRECTOR OF RELATIONS WITH SCHOOLS

DEAN OF THE MEDICAL SCHOOL

DEAN OF THE COLLEGE OF DENTISTRY

DIRECTOR OF UNIVERSITY EXTENSION

ADMINISTRATIVE SECRETARY

DEAN OF THE GRADUATE DIVISION *(Northern Section)*

MANAGER OF THE BUREAU OF GUIDANCE AND PLACEMENT

DIRECTOR OF THE INSTITUTE OF INDUSTRIAL RELATIONS *(Northern Section)*

DEAN OF THE SCHOOL OF NURSING

DEAN OF THE GRADUATE DIVISION *(Southern Section)*

COORDINATOR OF VETERANS' AFFAIRS

ASSISTANT TO THE PRESIDENT *(Public Information)*

DIRECTOR OF THE DIVISION OF VOCATIONAL EDUCATION

DEAN OF THE COLLEGE OF PHARMACY

CHIEF ACCOUNTING OFFICER

MANAGER OF THE UNIVERSITY PRESS

DIRECTOR OF THE INSTITUTE OF INDUSTRIAL RELATIONS *(Southern Section)*

DIRECTOR OF THE HOOPER FOUNDATION

DIRECTOR OF THE LICK OBSERVATORY

DIRECTOR OF WILMERDING SCHOOL

DIRECTOR OF THE CALIFORNIA SCHOOL OF FINE ARTS

DEAN OF THE HASTINGS COLLEGE OF LAW

BERKELEY CAMPUS*

26

gent services but runs counter to all good practice
if attempted in the literal terms of the By-Laws.[52]
It is perhaps no surprise that regents were taken aback to
see their performance so evaluated.

From this description of the board's detailed administrative activities, the report moved directly to an analysis
of the office of the president, noting that the description
in the Standing Orders that "The President of the University shall be the executive head of the University in all its
departments" was seriously contradicted in practice. Not
only were the secretary, treasurer, and attorney directly
responsible to the board, but the comptroller and a newly
appointed chief accounting officer reported both to the
board and the president.[53]

With reference to the president's direct activities, the
report repeated themes of the faculty committees four
years before, noting the existence of over 50 formal and
direct administrative channels to the president, including
20 resulting from the absence of a campus head at
Berkeley, following Monroe Deutsch's recent retirement:
"It is clearly apparent that lines of communication and
reporting to the President are numerous and that they
possess a baffling vagueness."[54] The president's workload
was also an object of concern—a monthly average of some
1,500 reports, letters, and other written materials requiring his personal attention; a continuous backlog of 200 to
500 matters awaiting decision, in addition to a normal
backlog of telephone calls and interviews. The report
concluded:

There is widespread agreement that distinguished
leadership and enormous expenditure of energy are
to be found in the President's office. Congestion of
University business, however, results in uncertainty and delay down through the administrative
channels. A flood of minor matters through the
office submerges consideration of major affairs.
There is, generally, a defensive retreat under the

protection of administrative minutiae rather than an offensive drive on broad policy fronts.[55]

The condition could be attributed, the report suggested, "to the impact of heavy new responsibilities upon administrative arrangements fashioned for days gone by," such as inadequate delegation by the regents to the president, conflicting delegation with respect to business affairs and accounting; insufficient intermediate administrative posts to which the president might delegate; and inadequate major staff assistance to the president.[56]

As had been requested, the survey team devoted considerable attention to the business and fiscal aspects of University administration, including the ambiguity of the relationship between the comptroller and the chief accounting officer. More critical to this essay, however, was the problem at the local level resulting from the direct reporting relationship between the comptroller and campus business managers who were responsible for such activities as grounds and buildings maintenance, purchasing and building construction:

> From the position of the Provost or other chief campus administrator, the existing situation is characterized by a serious lack of coordination and integration. Although such officials are ostensibly representatives of the President and responsible for the attainment of University teaching and research objectives, much locally important business flows around them.[57]

The same problem was identified concerning other functions administered directly by universitywide administrators, such as accounting, public information, and personnel.

With respect to the nominal heads of the several campuses, specifically the provost at UCLA, the report quoted the president's memorandum of April 8, 1946, cited above, noting that "a surface indication of large delegation and the creation of a powerful point of departure as to campus affairs . . . fades rapidly as an analysis is made of the realities of current practice." At Los Angeles, for example, 16 deans and administrative officers reported to the provost, but 15 other important offices, identified as "statewide departments," did not do so:

Not only does this pattern of administrative relationships reduce the authority of the Provost, but it tends to increase the problem of coordination on the campus level. . . . These and even more limitations on the adequate conduct of local affairs are observable on the other teaching campuses . . . [while] officials on the Berkeley campus are without the leadership and direction of a full-time superior and must await assistance on many campus problems from an already overloaded President.[58]

In summarizing the analysis, the report concluded:

—The Board of Regents . . . has burdened itself with review of operating details.

—[T]here is not a firm, uniformly applied concept as to division of responsibility as between the central office and the campuses, and the prevailing pattern of excessive centralization of authority over administrative detail precludes the expeditious transaction of campus business and inhibits the conduct of teaching and research.

—The provost or other campus head is not adequately empowered by delegation nor is he sufficiently in the flow of campus business to foster and facilitate a fully rounded campus program or to relieve the President and Regents of a burden of decisions as to campus affairs. In other words, the provost lacks both the responsibility and the staff for effective leadership as to campus curriculum, budget, personnel, accounting, and physical facilities.[59]

There was little in the survey team's analysis that had not been discussed in the comments and reports that had preceded their arrival, save perhaps the emphasis on re-

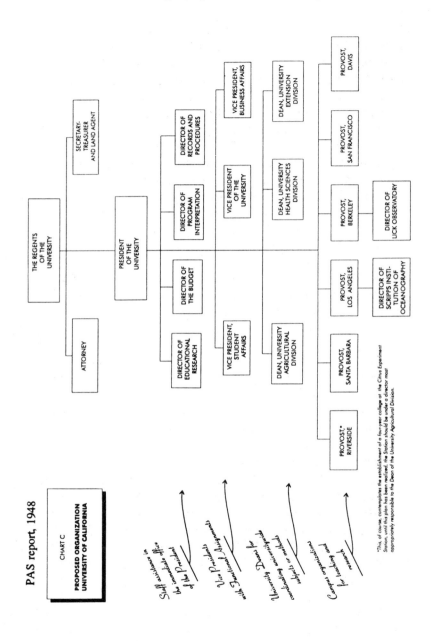

PAS report, 1948

CHART C

PROPOSED ORGANIZATION UNIVERSITY OF CALIFORNIA

THE REGENTS OF THE UNIVERSITY

SECRETARY-TREASURER AND LAND AGENT

ATTORNEY

PRESIDENT OF THE UNIVERSITY

DIRECTOR OF RECORDS AND PROCEDURES

DIRECTOR OF PROGRAM INTERPRETATION

DIRECTOR OF THE BUDGET

DIRECTOR OF EDUCATIONAL RESEARCH

VICE PRESIDENT, BUSINESS AFFAIRS

VICE PRESIDENT OF THE UNIVERSITY

VICE PRESIDENT, STUDENT AFFAIRS

DEAN, UNIVERSITY EXTENSION DIVISION

DEAN, UNIVERSITY HEALTH SCIENCES DIVISION

DEAN, UNIVERSITY AGRICULTURAL DIVISION

PROVOST, DAVIS

PROVOST, SAN FRANCISCO

PROVOST, BERKELEY

DIRECTOR OF LICK OBSERVATORY

PROVOST, LOS ANGELES

DIRECTOR OF SCRIPPS INSTITUTION OF OCEANOGRAPHY

PROVOST, SANTA BARBARA

PROVOST,* RIVERSIDE

Staff assistance in the immediate office of the President

Vice Presidents with Functional Assignments

Deans for University-wide coordinating subjects or related

Campus organizations for teaching and research

*This, of course, contemplates the establishment of a four-year college at the Citrus Experiment Station, until this plan has been realized, the Station should be under a director most appropriately responsible to the Dean of the University Agricultural Division.

30

gental involvement in administrative detail and the problems created by division of authority between the comptroller and the chief accounting officer. Indeed, the report's findings resembled the comments of Joel Hildebrand in 1943 and the Senate committees' conclusions of a year later. It was not surprising that the survey team's recommendations emerging from its analysis also bore strong resemblance to earlier faculty reports.

The recommendations began with a virtual paraphrase of the president's oft-stated principle to centralize policymaking and to decentralize execution of policies:

1. There must be unity in the University system.

2. There must be decentralization in University operations to the maximum extent compatible with unity.[60]

But the report's interpretation of the principle was far different from that of the president: "Attempts at remote control of campus affairs with a harvest of irritation and frustration contain seeds of horizontal separatism. . . . [T]he key to continuing growth and coordination of all parts of the University is in the office of the Provost." This position was to be established at each of the teaching campuses—Berkeley, Davis, San Francisco, and Santa Barbara, and at Riverside as that campus expanded.[61] Directors at Mt. Hamilton and La Jolla would have delegated authority, "so that local administrative matters may be handled expeditiously," but would receive assistance from the business offices and be under the general supervision of the provosts at Berkeley and Los Angeles, respectively.[62]

Subject to the overall policies of the regents and the general supervision of the president, the campus executive was to be granted sufficient authority to formulate and administer the campus budget, to appoint department chairmen and all nontenure faculty and to direct all campuswide aspects of public relations and student and business affairs. "These delegated duties should enable the Provost to render effective service to campus schools, colleges, departments, institutes, and bureaus."[63]

"Substantial delegations to the Provosts [would] relieve the President of a tremendous burden of detailed decisions [making time available] for planning, for conferring, and for providing even more effective leadership to the University."[64] If the president was to be, in fact, "the executive head of the University . . . and directly responsible for the organization and operation of the University," as set forth in the Standing Orders, there would have to be considerable delegation of authority by the regents. Officers concerned with matters of University administration—the comptroller and chief accounting officer—would have to be made responsible solely to the president. The president's authority would include approval of tenure appointments and promotions; the appointment of deans of schools and colleges and other campus officers reporting directly to the provost; appointment, subject to regent confirmation, of vice-presidents and provosts; and expanded authority to administer the University's budget, bringing only major changes to the regents.[65]

In addition to these basic responsibilities, the report suggested that the president's "fundamental contribution" to the University would be the development of long-range educational policies and programs, master plans for physical development, planning the basic administrative organization, and preparing the annual budget. "Through such activities," the report asserted, "there is limitless range for the President to meet his University obligations. From concentration on such activities will come opportunities for indispensable service and inspiring leadership from the President's office, factors which will be the most potent force for unity in the University system."[66]

To provide top-level assistance to the president, the report proposed the following key deputies: vice-president of the university, deans of university divisions (agriculture, extension, and health sciences), and vice-presidents for business and student affairs, the former incorporating the duties of the existing comptroller and chief accounting officer.[67]

The report turned again to the Board of Regents:
With generous delegation of authority from the Regents to the President of the University, and in turn down through the administrative organization, a new and more significant role is envisaged for this governing body, permitting maximum utilization of the rich talents of its members. The Regents will be able to concern themselves more fully with problems of major importance, including the formulation of general policies to guide the University, the determination of future expansions and contractions in the University's program, the general allocation of funds, and the accomplishment of the primary objectives of the University.[68]

Finally, in words that may well have distressed President Sproul, Class of 1913 and—with a one-year exception—a University employee and officer on the Berkeley campus ever since, the report proposed for consideration an "executive campus." Prophetic of events and developments that would not take place for decades, the report asked:
Can a Berkeley Provost exercise his full measure of responsibility with a President in close proximity? . . . Can the President provide the high leadership necessary if brought into day-to-day involvement, because of close geographical location, with the routine administrative problems of the individual campus? . . . [I]t is evident that physical attachment of the executive offices to any one campus might well lead to a distortion of the proposed administrative structure. . . . Consideration should be given, then, to actual physical separation of the executive offices from the administrative offices of any one campus. Such a separation, whether across the street or, better, miles distant, will serve

to identify and clarify the scope of responsibility of the President and his associates.[69]

COMMENTS AND CRITICISMS

Whether President Sproul was surprised by the tone and substance of the report is not clear. There is little question, however, that he did not wish the report to be widely distributed. One observer suggests that the president may have feared the negative publicity and possible state intrusion that could have followed public dissemination of the report.[70] Whatever the case, the report as a whole does not appear to have left the president's office—at least officially—until sent to the regents several months after its receipt. This was not because of a lack of interest. In a May 1948 commentary on a "Tentative-Confidential" outline of the proposed administration, director of university extension Baldwin Woods suggested to President Sproul that "the general report be released, when you consider desirable . . . so that the Administrative Committees of the Senate, both north and south, may be able to visualize the way in which academic administration fits into the over-all administrative plan."[71] Subsequently, the chair of UCLA's Senate committee on budget and interdepartmental relations asked, "Would it be possible for this committee, and perhaps other Senate committees such as the Committee on Committees and those on Educational Policy and University Reorganization, to study the report as a whole and to comment on it as it affects their special responsibilities?"[72] Joel Hildebrand, chair of the president's advisory committee at Berkeley, made a similar request to see the whole report because it dealt with "matters of deep concern to members of the faculty."[73]

The president chose a different course of action. In September 1948, the 139-page report was divided into its many sections, and excerpts were sent to specific officers. For example, the deans of schools and colleges were sent two pages concerning deans, statewide institute directors excerpts concerning their future role, deans of students a few paragraphs concerning the organization of student affairs, and so on. Significantly, the same distribution policy was followed with respect to the University's senior administrators, the comptroller, the provost and the vice-president of the University. In his cover letter to all of these officers, the president noted that the report was about ready for presentation to the regents and invited comment, "so that I may use them in the preparation of my own comments to the Regents upon the report as a whole."[74]

As might be expected, this procedure was questioned. Comptroller Corley noted that, "Because of missing pages, I may have misunderstood the intent of certain parts of the report."[75] Vice-President Hutchinson commented, "In studying the sections you have sent me I feel somewhat handicapped in not having before me the changes, if any, in the general form of University organization and administration which the Service may be proposing."[76] Provost Dykstra was more specific:

It is very difficult to tell much about the report from the materials which were sent to me. For illustration may I suggest that there is nothing in any of this material which has to do with the Office of the President or the Comptroller or the Regents and what is said about the Office of the Provost, without context, is partial and therefore a bit speculative."[77]

The comments, albeit fragmented, fell into several general areas. With respect to internal campus matters, one prominent incumbent suggested that the survey did not distinguish between the deans of single- and multi-departmental schools and colleges and the need for different allocations of authority to each.[78] A second and strongly worded memorandum from the chairman of Berkeley's Academic Senate committee on budget and interdepartmental relations took exception to the report's suggestion that, "Without adequate staff and facilities and in view of its composition, this committee is not well-equipped to second-guess responsible administrative officials. . . . [The committee should] emphasize policy and program aspects rather than details of positions of other specific items." "Taken together," wrote the Senate chairman,

> these passages amount to a summary condemnation of an institution by which the University of California has helped itself to grow great. They are a condemnation of the custom of allowing full and free collaboration between the administration and the faculty in the handling of the budget, down to the smallest details affecting immediately the work of academic departments.[79]

A third important comment concerned the disagreement of the chief accounting officer with the report's finding of "confusion" with respect to the pre-audit procedures and the independent postaudit, and the suggestion that the accounting function should be located within the purview of the vice-president, business affairs, rather than the existing dual reporting relationship to the president and to the regents. To the contrary, Olaf Lundberg suggested, "Fiscal control . . . can be discharged best and perhaps only under an organization which recognizes that the actions of the operating executive are subject to fiscal review and control, and, if need be, a veto."[80]

Other comments received by the president concerned such matters as the organization of student affairs, both on the campus and universitywide, budget preparation and university publications. Of much greater importance and central to this analysis, however, was the issue of the role of the chief campus executive *vis-à-vis* the president, the comptroller or vice-president, business affairs—the title recommended in the report—and statewide activities housed at the campus, such as agriculture.

The case for a strong campus executive, as recommended in the report, was clearly presented by Knowles Ryerson, long-time University faculty member, the senior administrator on the Davis campus, and a close personal associate of the president.

Ryerson appears to have been one of the few persons to have seen the full PAS report. In a hand-typed letter to President Sproul, written from his vacation home at Lake Tahoe in August 1948, Ryerson thanked the president for the opportunity to review "the tentative and confidential plan for university administration" and commented:

> It seems just good administration to give the administrative head on a campus single responsibility and authority to handle this campus within the broad policies laid down by the president and the regents. Then it is up to him to deliver—or get out. He should know where he stands, what his duties are and also his authority. I speak with some bias perhaps, but a ship can't be run with several different officers coming on the bridge, giving orders to various personnel without clearing with the skipper, much less advising him of what is being done. No steady course can be steered on that basis.

Writing from his vacation home at Echo Lake, President Sproul replied on August 17, 1948:

> As to your comments upon the Public Administration Survey report in its tentative form, I found them both penetrating and illuminating. . . . You may count on seeing the final report when it is ready.[81]*

Ryerson wrote to Sproul a month later:

---

*Sproul's reference to a "final" report is not clear but perhaps refers to his intended personal commentary to the regents concerning the PAS study.

Figure 10: Knowles Ryerson, 1948.

After eleven years on this campus endeavoring to coordinate activities without having definite responsibilities or adequate information as to what University policies might be, I see no answer to the problem of effective administration except delegation of authority with strict accountability for results. Prestige soon loses any high octane content it might have if not backed up by tangible authority to act. Figureheads should have no place in a well-organized administration. It hurts to hear the not uncommon, but well intended remark often made to me—"I know I should go through you, but I also know you haven't any authority, so it's quicker to deal directly with Berkeley. But I don't envy your position."

[Creating an effective provost] will free the top University executives from multitudinous detail and allow more time and thought for over-all statewide policy and the anticipation of changing conditions in the state and nation that will have an impact upon the University.[82]

The comments of Provost Dykstra, writing in September 1948 of his experience as nominal head of the Los Angeles campus for the previous three and one-half years, were more explicit. After noting the report's reference to the president's memorandum of April 16, 1945 cited above, concerning the provost's authority, Dykstra observed:

My comment would be the one which I have made to you from time to time that to date the directive has not worked out as contemplated for several reasons, some of which these commenters point out. For instance, I am much less sure than I was in February of 1945 that a Provost can go very far in the field of recruitment or of the canvass of talent without frequently getting himself into the position of having to seem to commit himself before he can do so. With the best will in the world it becomes physically impossible for the Provost to advise the President as to the status of personnel negotiations if they are to proceed while the President is in the East for several weeks. . . . It has been impossible also to make the Chairmen of Departments believe that the Provost has authority without taking those questions to the Office of the President. . . . One of the most trying situations in which to be when asked by a Dean or a Department Chairman, for instance, whether "We can go out and look for instructor material" is to be able to say only, "We shall need further authority to do this". . . . I cannot believe that the President should be bothered or that the Regents should be troubled with the shifting of minor budgetary items or the determination, for instance, to appoint an instructor and a teaching assistant for a semester instead of an assistant professor because the professor cannot be found at the moment. . . .

I would like very much to know what the reporters have to say about the relations between the Regents and the President and it is my great hope that something may be done to release the President from some of the manacles which, as I see it, now fetter him and prevent him from taking prompt action on some matters.[83]*

---

*A UCLA professor recalled a similar comment from Provost Dykstra:

I remember Dykstra saying one thing to me one time. He says, "Cliff, remember I used to tell you I was worried why Sproul wouldn't give me certain powers? . . . He doesn't have them." This was in the period when the Regents and Sproul were getting to be a little at odds. . . . Sproul just could not do some of those things. The Regents wanted to keep that power.[84]

Provost Dykstra's views were deeply held. In her oral history, Hansena Frederickson, executive secretary to UCLA's provosts and chancellors from 1936 to 1966, recalled:

Provost Dykstra was the most frustrated of all the chief campus officers because he came from the presidency of a big university, the University of Wisconsin, to the provostship here. He was called Vice President and Provost, and he didn't have the authority to do anything. He couldn't talk to the Regents; he was just so frustrated. He couldn't get to Sproul. At times, Dr. Sproul would be sitting on something vital and important to the campus, and we couldn't get through by phone to him for days and days.[85]*

A specific issue of concern to Ryerson and Dykstra was the relation of the campus executive to nonacademic matters. Ryerson commented:

---

*Two other senior UCLA officers commented in a similar fashion:

[Dykstra] would come and tell me, oh dozens of times, how he had tried to get the president's office in Berkeley to get something cleared up, but usually could get no response, then it would seem to him that inaction prevailed, and just dragged on and on and on.[86]

There was real coolness between [Dykstra and Sproul] during that entire time [1945-50]. . . . [Dykstra] would relate the many times that he'd written to Berkeley, to Sproul, or to other offices in the statewide headquarters and received no answer. Occasionally his authority would be undercut; he would make proposals on things, and they would be turned down by Berkeley. . . . He apparently saw very clearly, even in those days, that UCLA needed the autonomy which it now has, and that the chancellor needed freedom to do a proper job. . . . [H]e'd had the background and experience to make his own decisions. And when he was undercut by Berkeley it was just too much for him.[87]

Each major campus involves a varied range of business enterprises and activities. The report rightly recognizes their vital importance in relation to the proposed duties of the Provost. The proposed Business Affairs officer will be the right hand of the Provost in handling the different activities enumerated. Regardless of who holds the positions of head of a campus and of business manager and no matter how closely they work together, the present system of involving independent offices each responsible to separate offices in Berkeley has not and cannot result in a well-coordinated program.[88]

Provost Dykstra added a specific example:

This morning, for instance, I have a letter from the Comptroller of the University which has to do with the assignment of space on this campus and suggesting that certain priority be given to Geophysics as soon as the Art Department is taken care of by a proposal made from this campus. It would seem to me that the Comptroller would easily agree that someone on this campus is in better position to act on such a matter than someone sent from his office in Berkeley to investigate. . . . As I have indicated to you before it seems to me that a local business officer could do much to facilitate the operations on the campus if he is not too fearful that his wrists will be slapped because he is exercising some independence. . . . [T]here is in a great many offices which answer elsewhere the constant and reiterated query "what will Berkeley say?"[89]

Comptroller Corley held the opposite view:

It would appear to me that one of the major policies adopted by most business organizations and in effect at the University of California has been practically abolished in the suggestions of the P.A.S., namely the check and balance system. It appears that the academic head of each campus will have the responsibility for dictating the business operations as well as the academic operations. If my interpretation of the recommendations is correct, I believe the report is fundamentally unsound on that basis, as all organizations find it necessary to have some control on the expenditures of its funds with a policy set definitely by a business administrator. . . . I approve both coordination and local responsibility with the Provost on each campus but not direction and dictation of operations and policies.[90]*

The chief accounting officer, Olaf Lundberg, was equally critical. In a letter to the president he commented on a memorandum from a PAS staff member:

Mr. Clapp also states that I am "hesitant in relinquishing direct control over the local accounting offices." He is correct in this statement, and I might perhaps point out that my hesitancy stems

---

*In a 1967 oral interview, Vice President Corley expanded on this view:

Campuses are localized to serve the people, but the responsibility of the management and operation and fiscal affairs, as well as the general policy, rests with the Regents as a trust for the state. It is only given to them as a trust. I think people of the state look upon the Regents and the President to guide the campuses, let them run their show from an academic point of view, but the general relationships and management and operation, including the policies on the campus, should be approved by the President and the Regents. . . . I believe in a centralized University system allowing sufficient independence on the campuses for them to run their campus within the scope of the policy set by the President and the Regents, and without interference, but with sufficient controls that they can't be recognized as the local agency serving that section of the state.[91]

from knowledge hard bought, not taught. . . . It hardly seems necessary to remind you of the lack of uniformity and standardization which existed when there was no central administrative control over the University-wide accounting functions. As the University grew in size and complexity, this defect led to a breakdown in fiscal control which necessitated a complete reorganization, and, incidentally, is the reason for my being here today.[92]

Herman Spindt, the statewide director of admissions, responded negatively to the report's assertion that the separation of the local admissions office from the campus structure was a "major weakness." He reiterated his position that uniform admission requirements should be the responsibility of a universitywide officer:

[I]t is my belief that the separation . . . is a source of strength rather than weakness. Pressure on local administrative officers and on local admissions officers is less under a University-wide administration. . . . [93]

Clearly, for these three universitywide officers, there was little confidence in the decentralized university system recommended by the report. For Claude Hutchinson, vice-president and dean of the universitywide college of agriculture, the problem was more complicated. He expressed general support for

somewhat autonomous and independent campuses . . . provided there can be at the same time . . . special provisions for strong chains between those campuses on which related activities exist . . . in the case of agriculture four campuses, without doing violence to campus organization. . . . The only question is how far campus and Provost authority can be carried without doing violence to University unity, and in some instances such as agriculture, forestry, home economics, and veterinary science which overlap campuses, to coordination and cooperation between related fields and segments of the same field.[94]

The committee appointed by the president to study the expansion of Riverside and Davis used similar language in its report on September 7, 1948:

While the magnitude of the expansion proposed must bring to these campuses certain administrative and academic autonomy . . . no barriers need to develop which might interfere with existing relationships between Berkeley and Davis. . . . [S]imilar relationships should be fostered between the Los Angeles and Riverside campuses. Such relationships should result in unifying and strengthening the University fabric between its major and outlying campuses, as well as between its northern and southern sections. [Business affairs units should] work with the Provost . . . as to the execution of policies.[95]

A similar issue was presented in connection with the report's recommendation for the appointment of a universitywide dean for the health sciences to serve as an advisor to the president, but only in a coordinating capacity with respect to campus officials. Dean of Public Health Edward Rogers, responsible for programs at both Berkeley and Los Angeles, expressed concern:

If we have truly universitywide areas of opportunity where unity in purpose, plan and program are essential, where university leadership (in a sociological sense) is indicated, then I believe they should be firmly planted as universitywide functions and administered as such.[96]

The ball was in the president's court. Although the comments he had received were based on the same evidence, there was little consensus. The advice he had requested was contradictory.* The reality behind the rhetoric of "centralized policy-making" and "decentralized policy-execution" continued to be ambiguous. As had been suggested by several of the commentators and emphasized in the report, little could be done unless the regents delegated much of their authority to the president. But it was uncertain whether this was high on the president's priority list. If the regents did not delegate, he would continue to be involved in the administrative detail that filled the regents' agenda, detail with which he clearly felt comfortable and confident and requiring a uniformity of approach that he could personally provide and in which he believed. What Dykstra described as "manacles" was for Sproul the *raison d'être* for his management style and protective of the unity of the university, his paramount concern.

THE REGENTS' REVIEW:
THE CENTRAL ADMINISTRATION

Nine months after its delivery to the president in mid-1948, the PAS report went to the regents. While the

---

*One comment sent to the president questioned the objectivity of at least one member of the survey team. In a handwritten personal note to President Sproul written on September 9, 1948, Professor Robert Webb, then at the Santa Barbara campus, noted that

> An assistant in the P.A.S. entrusted with much of the Los Angeles campus interviewing is the son of the Dean of the School of Education, Los Angeles, who, in my opinion, was steeped from childhood in the myth of Berkeley domination and blocking of Los Angeles activities. I therefore place little confidence in the sincereness (sic.) or accuracy of P.A.S. findings.

Webb's concerns came as a considerable surprise to me on learning some 44 years later that, as a young graduate assistant on the P.A.S. team, I had been credited with such influence![97]

Eugene C. Lee

Figure 11: Meeting of UC Regents, August 1950; Sproul speaking, Underhill with back to the camera, Canaday seated center facing camera, Neylan far end of the table.

47

president had received comments from various persons within the University to whom he had sent excerpts of the report, there is no evidence of additional activity during this period. Indeed, the report seemed to have disappeared. As if to reassure his senior associates that this was not the case, the president informed them in March 1949 that the report was "still alive, and its recommendations would lead to administrative changes."[98]

There would be a long wait. The regents' consideration of the report continued for two years, during which time much of their attention was devoted to the loyalty oath controversy that engulfed the University from 1949 to 1952.[99] And in the consideration of the report that did take place, they virtually ignored its fundamental finding that "the key to continuing growth and coordination of all parts of the University is in the office of the Provost." In fact, not until after the death of Provost Dykstra in May 1950 was the role of the campus executive even considered. In retrospect, both the president and the regents, undoubtedly preoccupied by the issue of the oath, seemed unable to move beyond the basic authority structure that they felt had served the University so well up to that time.

No evidence has been found that the regents were aware of the earlier faculty committee reports and the comments received by the president, or that they made any effort to obtain independent evaluations of the PAS study. Instead their initial reaction to the report was to repudiate it. Writing in April 1949, one member of the board expressed "shock" over the report's "very critical attitude [toward] the alleged failure of the Regents to delegate authority to the President and of the President in turn to delegate administrative authority, particularly to Deans and Provosts on the various campuses of the University . . . who are primarily college professors . . . notorious for their lack of business ability."[100]

A special committee of the board was appointed to review the survey. At the group's first meeting in June

1949, the president made clear his disagreement with the
report in words reminiscent of his 1943 response to Joel
Hildebrand's Academic Senate speech. The solution to the
University's administrative problems was not, the president suggested, to divorce the central administration from
the operation of its campuses, "setting up the Provosts as
practically independent officers"—as he characterized the
report's recommendation, but to strengthen the central
administration. The appointment of a vice-president of
the University, a vice-president for medical and health
sciences, and two additional officers—one to prepare the
university's budget, the other to supervise contract
research activities, would relieve the "almost intolerable
burdens" on his office that had "resulted in an unfortu-
nate congestion and some retardation of University
business." A vice-president for business affairs (the
existing comptroller) would be responsible to the president, while the chief accounting officer would be made
solely responsible to the regents.

As for the chief campus executive, the president's
words explicitly revealed his personal philosophy: "[T]he
Provost would become of relatively less importance in
general University affairs, but would have fully adequate
authority in what might be called "campus housekeeping,
in local public relations, and in local administration
generally." "Campus housekeeping" was *not* what the
PAS or faculty reports had envisaged.[101]

As recorded at a committee meeting in February 1950,
Regent Dickson went even further in opposing the continuance of the office of provost:

> The office is a menace to the unity of the Universi-
> ty in that it places such local responsibilities in one
> man that the position of the President is given
> secondary recognition on the campus. It gives
> emphasis to a feeling of local autonomy, and under
> the leadership of a provost with personal ambitions
> might conceivably lead to a movement for separa-
> tion. Further [Dickson stated] that even under the

best conditions the students and community develop a sentiment toward their local officer which often results in a resentment of powers exercised by the President or other state-wide officers.

It was Regent Dickson's recommendation that [as he had suggested in 1947] in the place of a provost, the administration of each local campus be under the supervision of a committee of three [senior faculty], one of whom, the chairman, would act full time, and the other two would treat the appointment as an additional duty to their teaching programs, meeting with the chairman perhaps once a week, or more often if emergency problems should arise. . . . He said that this arrangement had been successful at the California Institute of Technology.[102]

President Sproul responded that, after giving the matter considerable thought, "[W]hile the committee would clear away one great evil, that is, the feeling of resentment toward the powers exercised by the President, he had come to the conclusion that it would be better to have a chief executive officer with fixed responsibilities." Regent Griffiths then noted that the committee arrangement was no longer in effect at Cal Tech.[103]

The regents did not agree that they devoted too much attention to detail. The criticism was "not well founded." The president concurred: "[T]he Board cannot deal only in generalities, and it is good practice for executives to report to the Board . . . in advance of action." Regent John Francis Neylan, a prominent attorney, stressed the role of regents as trustees, "who have been given responsibilities which cannot be delegated."[104*]

---

*Robert S. Johnson comments:
John Neylan, in particular, had the lawyer's idea that, as the state constitution stated, the university was a

In the regents' review of University organization, the discussion up to mid-1950 focused almost entirely on the structure of the central administration and only rarely referred to the PAS report. A major and continuing topic was the reporting relationship of the vice-president, business affairs. Regent Neylan, increasingly at odds with the president,* insisted that the vice-president be responsible directly to the board. The president disagreed, stressing that his responsibilities as executive head of the University must include business activities. Finally, a dual reporting relationship was accepted. The establishment of a vice-president of the University was confirmed by the board in September 1949, although the office was not filled until 1958.** Two vice-presidencies, for agricultural

---

"public trust" and that as trustees the Board of Regents had to administer it directly. This idea had come down from the early days of the university's history. . . . [E]ven down into Sproul's term the regents maintained that they had to give final approval to everything: all budget transfers, all new appointments and promotions and salary increases.[105]

*President Emeritus David Gardner writes:
Regent Neylan and President Sproul had been close personal friends for years and had worked together harmoniously. But for whatever reasons—the burden of business after World War II, the number of new appointments to the Board, the overwhelming number of matters pending—Neylan and Sproul by 1949 were less cordial than before. Where the relationship between Neylan and Sproul had been a source of stability between the office of the President and the Board of Regents, it was by the time of the oath a potentially disruptive factor.[106]

**At the February 1950 meeting of the regents committee on reorganization, the president reported on the creation of a faculty search committee for the position of vice-president of the University and indicated that an appointment effective July 1, 1950, was anticipated. The regents briefly reviewed the persons

sciences and university extension, involving primarily changes in title, were approved by the board in February 1950, the former to take effect upon the forthcoming retirement of Claude Hutchinson, vice-president and dean of the college of agriculture. The president's recommendation to establish a vice-president for medical science was deferred.[108]

In summary, in 1950, two years after its completion, the Public Administration Service report had been seen in its entirety—officially at least—by only the president and the regents. The report had had little influence on the University's administrative structure.

This was to change.

THE REGENTS' REVIEW:
THE ROLE OF THE CHANCELLOR

The continued vacancy in the Berkeley provostship following Monroe Deutsch's retirement in 1947 does not appear to have engendered much concern.* In contrast, the death of Provost Dykstra in 1950 and the question of his replacement at UCLA threw into high profile the

---

under consideration and "agreed there were many outstanding men on the list."[107] No appointment was to take place for eight years.

*Late in 1949, President Sproul wrote to the chairman of the Academic Senate's northern section committee on committees, asking for the appointment of a special committee to advise the president as to suitable candidates for the position of provost at the Berkeley campus. Although the minutes of the regents give no indication of discussion of this matter, the president commented that "The special committee of the Regents which is studying the administrative structure and procedures of the University has now gone far enough to justify the conclusion that there will be a Provost on the Berkeley campus."[109] In any event, the next campus head at Berkeley, Clark Kerr, was not appointed until 1952.

strains under which the centralized university structure was operating. One wonders, in fact, how long consideration of this issue would have been deferred if the Los Angeles vacancy had not occurred. It is quite possible that the office of chancellor would not have been created until after President Sproul's retirement in 1958. Paradoxically, it was Dykstra's death that precipitated the events that led to the administrative changes he had so long espoused. The president and the regents were forced to come to grips with the issue of campus leadership. The PAS study, which had all but disappeared from view, was resurrected.

The change in climate was initiated by an informal meeting of southern California regents to discuss the UCLA vacancy, following which the chairman of the board appointed a subcommittee to make procedural recommendations. The committee was chaired by a new regent, John Canaday, who had a particular interest in the problems of the Los Angeles campus and a background in large-scale organization as an executive of the Lockheed Corporation.

In making its report to the regents' committee on southern California schools, colleges, and institutions in October 1950, the subcommittee emphasized that it had "carefully perused" the "comprehensive" PAS study and had "drawn heavily on its findings and recommendations."[110] No reference was made to the disparaging remarks that had characterized previous discussions of the report.

The subcommittee reported that the need for a fundamental change in administrative procedures affecting UCLA had been apparent and growing for the past 20 years and that, in fact, the situation appeared to be "more critical than at any previous time." Specifically, the three regents observed, it would be "difficult, if not impossible" for the University to attract a person of high caliber to the UCLA post unless there was a clarification of "lines of authority and responsibility." The subcommittee cited the

PAS report at great length, unequivocally endorsing its recommendation concerning the provostship but ignoring the report's call for regental delegation of authority to the president and downward to the campus. That there was an inherent inconsistency between a strong campus executive and a board heavily involved in administrative detail was not mentioned and perhaps not recognized.

The subcommittee's report required that President Sproul deal with the PAS survey. In his statement to the subcommittee, he reviewed the historic record of regents' actions noted above—its 1937 endorsement of a "centralized administration," its 1943 action describing the provost's scope of authority but stressing central control and the April 1946 memorandum that had been cited in the PAS report and repeated by the subcommittee. In an uncharacteristically defensive tone, the president described some of the PAS findings cited by the subcommittee as inaccurate and reported that "many" of the report's recommendations had been adopted. For example, the report had cited 50 administrative channels to the president but, Sproul stated, there were now only 25. With reference to his "unreasonable" workload, the president noted that three vice-presidents had been appointed (only two were in place and these represented merely a change in title). The administration of public relations had been decentralized, and the personnel office was in process of decentralization. He challenged the report's assertion of his involvement in detailed campus administration, stating that he had "not for years discussed departmental business with a department chairman."[111]

Turning to the subcommittee's recommendations, the president asserted that "The Los Angeles campus now has administrative and operating autonomy along the general lines recommended in the P.A.S. report." This was an over-statement that went unchallenged, but the president did observe that "A clearer definition of responsibilities and authority is evidently desirable." He expressed strong opposition to the proposed changes in title—from provost to president and from president to chancellor—indicating that this would set the stage for converting the University to a "loosely knit federation of institutions without strong leadership." In response to the recommendation that the provosts (Berkeley and Los Angeles) attend regents' meetings, the president indicated that he now invited them when "their important problems are under discussion . . . thus making clear the fact that they appear before the Regents as aides to the President in the presentation of the Administration's program, and not as of right and as independent officers." The president stated his agreement with the suggestion that the local campus executive "should be established in the public mind as more than the titular heads of their respective campuses" and observed that there had been "regrettable departures" from this practice in the past. He indicated, however, his intention to continue to preside at commencement and charter day exercises. Finally, the president took strong exception to the proposal that a subcommittee of the regents conduct the search for a successor to the late Provost Dykstra: the president's "chief assistants should not be appointed otherwise than upon his nomination."[112]

For the next three months, a major object of regental discussion and debate concerned the role of the chief campus executive. Although the focus was almost entirely on the vacancy at Los Angeles, it was clear that whatever was decided for UCLA would also apply to Berkeley and had implications for the smaller campuses as well. Surprisingly, although the PAS survey provided the springboard for the discussion, as evidenced by the regents' subcommittee report, the principal concerns of the president and the regents involved issues that the survey team had only briefly, if at all, considered. These were questions of title, who was to preside at University ceremonies, and who was to attend regents' meetings. In contrast, the issue of the authority and responsibility of the campus executive, specifically his jurisdiction over business affairs, was scarcely discussed.

A change of title had to be considered, indicated Regent Canaday, the spokesman for the Los Angeles position, because "provost" was too attached to the past "administrative deficiencies" of that campus. President Sproul proposed "chancellor," but Canaday pressed for a reversal of titles. The heads of Berkeley and Los Angeles should be designated "presidents," while the systemwide head should be "chancellor."* Sproul objected: It would be interpreted as "kicking the president upstairs." Regent Nimitz, the distinguished admiral of World War II fame, proposed "president-general" for the university and "president of the University of California at Berkeley or Los Angeles" for the respective campus heads. Regent Neylan concluded:

> [T]he most important acid test is what is the fellow going to think that you offer the job to. . . . If this campus is to have autonomy and if it is to be real, you have to give them the habiliments that go with autonomy. You cannot dress the doll up and call it something and have it look differently. It all comes back to whether we are going to go for real autonomy or not. . . . All are united on the theory of the highest degree of autonomy consistent with a unified university. . . . Basically that is the issue.[113]

That the issue of "autonomy" involved far more than title was not raised. In January 1951, the title of "chancellor" was accepted for the Berkeley and Los Angeles campuses. There was no suggestion that the title or expanded role should apply to other campuses of the University, a

---

*This would, of course, have required an amendment to the state constitution, involving both legislative action and a vote of the people. Surprisingly, this fact was not discussed by the regents.

continuance of "provost" apparently being taken for granted.*

Who should preside at charter day and commencement at the campuses was a second issue of major concern, with the president placing great emphasis on the symbolism of his appearance as head of the entire University. In contrast, Regent Canaday stressed the need to dignify the campus executive in the public eye as "head of the campus in fact as well as in title." After much discussion, compromise language was adopted providing that the campus head would preside at all formal functions and "present" the president at commencement and charter day ceremonies, who—"as the university's chief executive"—would function in accordance with the University's rules for protocol and procedure, rules that were yet to be formulated.[114]

A third issue involved the attendance of the two chancellors at regents' meetings. Would they attend as a matter of right or only on specific invitation of the president? The eventual compromise provided that the president "shall invite," leaving him in the formal picture but eliminating his discretion except for committee meetings of the board.[115] In contrast, other campus heads—provosts and directors—could or could not be invited at the president's discretion.

On the responsibility of the campus executive over business affairs, a major issue in the PAS survey as it had been in the earlier faculty reports, the president was silent. Having lost the debate, primarily to Regent Neylan, over the direct reporting relationship of the vice-

---

*As of 1950, the title of provost was also in use at the Riverside and Santa Barbara campuses and was extended to the Davis campus in 1952. In 1958, these provosts were designated as chancellors, which was also the title used at Santa Cruz, Irvine, and San Diego as these campuses were established in the early 1960s. At San Francisco, the provost title was first used in 1958 and was changed to chancellor in 1964.

president, business affairs to the Board of Regents, the president appears to have been willing to let this issue be resolved without his recommendation. Regent Canaday expressed concern over the lack of local authority but, perhaps counting votes on the board, failed to press the matter.[116] The end result was a continuation of the ambiguity that had plagued Provost Dykstra and Dean Ryerson. The revised Regents' Standing Orders adopted in March 1951 provided that the campus executive was the executive head of all activities on the campus, excluding business affairs (and other statewide offices), but in contradictory fashion gave him administrative authority over business operations consistent with policies determined by the vice-president, business affairs.

A notice in the April 1951 *Faculty Bulletin* summarized the regents' actions. "The reorganization is designed to do three things," explained President Sproul: "streamline the administrative machinery" of the University; "define clearly the duties of the various University officers"; and "give to each of the eight campuses within the state-wide University the maximum degree of autonomy consistent with unity." The chancellors at Berkeley and Los Angeles, and the several vice-presidents were to be "the top-level administrative officers under the president," and the vice-president, business affairs was also to be responsible to the regents. Duties of the chancellors and other chief campus heads (provosts and directors) included the nomination through the president of all faculty and administrative personnel and the executive direction of all activities on their campuses "except those of a state-wide nature."[117]

The announcement stated that the two chancellors would attend regents' meetings and preside at formal functions, as described above. However, that little had really changed in terms of decentralization of authority to the campus was indicated by the following statement: "The duties of the President are essentially the same as they have been for many years. As executive head of the

University of California he is directly responsible for its
organization and operation, its internal administration,
and the care of its grounds and property." President
Sproul's belief in a "centralized administration," first
enunciated in 1937, remained unshaken. Only with
chancellors actually in place in 1952 would this belief be
challenged.

EPILOGUE

Not all changes announced in April 1951 were immediately implemented. In fact, amendments to the reorganization package were soon suggested. In January 1952, the president discussed with the regents a joint appointment whereby Raymond Allen, the chancellor-elect at Los Angeles and a medical doctor, would also serve as vice-president, medical sciences.[118] However, the whole issue of a medical vice-presidency was postponed; the position was not filled until 1955.

Similarly, while the president had indicated in January 1952 (as he had in 1950) that he would nominate a person to be vice-president of the University "in the near future," Regent Neylan questioned the need for the position "in view of the Chancellor appointments just made and in view of the powers which the Chancellors are to exercise."[119] As noted above, the position was not filled until after the president's retirement in 1958. Of the other vice-presidencies, business affairs and university extension involved only title changes; the post of vice-president, agricultural-sciences was filled in 1952.

In 1955, the University's administrative structure was again reviewed, as part of the "Restudy of the Needs of California in Higher Education," known as the McConnell Report.[120] Authorized by the legislature in 1953, the report, prepared for the liaison committee of the Board of Regents and the State Board of Education, was an exhaustive analysis of the programs, plans, and organizational structure of the University, and the state and junior college systems. This time the report was made public.

Without reference and while acknowledging recent changes, the McConnell Report basically repeated and confirmed the findings and recommendations of the Public

Administration Service study of 1948. While the Board of Regents had "made commendable progress" in freeing its docket from unnecessary detail—for example, delegating to the president the power to approve transfers within subdivisions of a departmental budget and allowing him to approve transfers, not to exceed $3,000 each, from contingency funds—if the regents were "to save time for their most important functions, as they undoubtedly should, they must . . . drastically [reduce] the number of items on which they take detailed action. . . . Only by confining their activities to policy-making and review in such matters as these and by leaving their administration to proper officers can the Regents free themselves for their essential responsibilities."[121]

With respect to the president, the report concluded that "The University's administrative procedures and decisions could be made even more efficiently and promptly if . . . the Regents were to broaden the scope of the President's authority." But he, too, should "free himself from routine operating details [by] systematic decentralization of operating functions among the several campuses".[122]

This means that State-wide offices or officers should not be burdened with the day-to-day administrative operations of the several campuses, institutes, or research laboratories, but that the authority and responsibility for conducting these activities and operations should be delegated to the administrative heads of these units. The only exceptions to this division of authority should be those which are demonstrably more efficiently and economically conducted centrally."[123]

The restudy staff commended the president "for having made considerable progress in the formal decentralization of administrative powers and responsibilities to the heads of the several campuses." For example, department heads were now directly responsible to the chief campus officer, and the campus business manager had a "line relationship" to the campus head (the end result of extensive negotiations between the two new chancellors, Raymond Allen and Clark Kerr, and vice-president, business affairs James Corley). But the report noted that several programs on the campuses—accounting, nonacademic personnel, purchasing, plant planning, and construction—were still under the administrative direction of "statewide" officers and that even for the functions that had been reassigned, "It remains to make the delegation [of authority to the campuses] more effective in practice. Long-time habits of action on campus matters, particularly at Berkeley, in the President's office are difficult to break, but should be resolutely put aside."[124] As Robert Johnson noted, many of the administrative actions of the chancellors and other campus heads continued to be subject to detailed central review.

> The trouble lay in the [requirement that campuses act] "within approved policy." Because this was not always spelled out clearly, local officers would have, very often, to get in touch with the central administration to find out the policies and how they were to be interpreted. In effect, the central offices were still calling too many shots.[125]

Thus, by the mid-1950s there had been important developments in the University's administrative organization. But for the regents, the president, and many of his senior colleagues, changes of the magnitude proposed in the Public Administration Service report involved too abrupt a departure from policies and practices with which they felt familiar and that, they believed, had served the University well and, indeed, had held it together. Years of interpersonal relationships and ways of doing business were not to be set aside quickly, despite the pressures of institutional expansion that the university confronted. Indeed, the extraordinary capacity and energy of the president enabled him to follow old and accepted patterns of administration and to put aside calls for change, even as the changes became inevitable. For President Sproul,

Figure 12: Chancellor Kerr and President Sproul, 1954 (at the dedication of the Alumni House).

the unity of the University was not to be compromised by an untested scheme of decentralization.

To embark on a different administrative course would require new faces, indeed a generational shift, both on the governing board and in the presidency. Only after Chancellor Kerr became president in 1958 was the chancellors' responsibility for campus administrative units clearly established. And not until 1966, under pressure from the now nine chancellors, did the regents delegate to the president, and he in turn to the chancellors, a full measure of authority for campus administration. A new balance of campus autonomy within a unified university was struck.[126] After the passage of more than 20 years, Joel Hildebrand's 1943 statement of principle and the faculty's recommendations of 1944 were finally implemented. How that happened is another story, waiting to be told.

AFTERWORD

Eugene C. Lee's excellent monograph, *The Origins of the Chancellorship*, is a beautifully told tale of the lengthy and difficult history leading up to the creation of that title with all the authority and privileges pertaining thereto. As one who has been a beneficiary of that action, and a participant-observer in almost all of the subsequent history of the University of California, I read and re-read it with great interest. The title of Lee's work is both descriptive and misleading. It is, of course, an accurate and detailed account of the origins of the critical position of chancellor as the executive of the several campuses of the University. But it also chronicles, as Clark Kerr noted in his foreword, "the early years . . . of what turned out to be a more than a twenty-year reorganization process . . . of the University of California."

A word about my roles as beneficiary and participant-observer might serve to illuminate the vantage point from which I offer the ensuing commentary.

As a student at UC Riverside in the first class accepted there (1954), I served as the first student body president, under the founder and initial provost, Gordon Watkins. This was the period in which chancellors (and to a lesser extent provosts) were delegated limited authority to manage some of the academic affairs of the campuses; the business, financial, and many student matters were the responsibility of managers on the campuses who reported to vice-presidents, comptrollers, and directors.

During the last three years of the Robert Gordon Sproul administration (from Fall 1955 to Fall 1958), I was a graduate student in the UCLA political science department, serving as a teaching assistant and an analyst in the Bureau of Governmental Research. I was also very active in the re-creation of the Graduate Student Association and, in that capacity, had an opportunity (as I had earlier at Riverside) to observe closely the operation of the several parts of the campus administration in relation to each other, as well as *vis-à-vis* the central administration then resident on the Berkeley campus.

Following a year in Washington, D.C., as an American Political Science Association Congressional Fellow, I was invited to accept a joint position as assistant professor of political science at UC Davis and as administrative analyst in the office of Clark Kerr, who was just beginning his second year as president of the University of California. My year in this dual capacity coincided with the development and finalization of the *Master Plan for Higher Education* and the beginning stages of the formulation of *The Growth Plan for the University of California*, efforts that precluded any intensive effort at continued administrative decentralization and reorganization. However, just prior to my leaving Berkeley in 1960 to come to UCLA as assistant to the chancellor and assistant professor of political science, a comprehensive report on the organization and management of the University, which had been commissioned by the regents at the recommendation of Kerr a year earlier, was completed. I had the opportunity to do some of the early staff work based on those recommendations, which served as the touchstone of the second phase of the 20-year reorganization of the University.

That, as Lee says in his concluding remarks, is the beginning of "another story, waiting to be told." It is, however, a story in which I played a part. I served from 1960-68 in a variety of positions from assistant to the chancellor to administrative vice-chancellor under the new chancellor of UCLA, the late Franklin D. Murphy who, to understate the case, was the major force pressing for greater decentralization, which finally came about in 1966. This added delegation came just in time for my transition to the position of chancellor of UCLA in 1968, a role I have been playing for the 26 years since.

Having provided the outlook from which my conclusions are formed, the following comments seem to me to be most pertinent in placing the fascinating story of *The Origins of the Chancellorship* in perspective. Although Lee is overly reticent on this point, due undoubtedly to his personal role in the process, the study and report of the PAS Survey is, in my view, the *sine qua non* of all subsequent decentralization of the University. While few of its recommendations were implemented in 1952, and while much more needed to be accomplished in order to get the University through the post-Sproul period, two things about it stand out in relation to the long-term course of the University's history.

First, given the experience, attitude, and aptitude of Sproul and those who were his colleagues in the universitywide administration, no substantial changes in the structure or governance of the University could have been conceived without the impetus of a set of external recommendations such as those emanating from the report. Indeed, as is clear from reading the responses of Sproul, Corley, Lundberg, Spindt, *et al.*, quoted in the body of this work, each would have preferred that the report not see the light of day. It was only the Board of Regents, led by those members who had a special concern for and understanding of the needs and problems faced by the Los Angeles campus, who were able to get the report's recommendations for the creation of a real campus executive with delegated authority from the president (though clearly not any of the recommendations dealing with reduced authority and responsibility of the regents) before the board for action.

Second, the most critical of the recommendations for the future restructuring and decentralization of the University of California was the creation of a chief campus executive with, as Regent Neyland said, "the habiliments that go with autonomy." Once that was done, whatever the intent of President Sproul and some of the regents, the seeds of destruction of the centralized system that had governed the University during the first 85 years of its existence had been planted. Without those changes Clark Kerr could never have been installed as chancellor of the Berkeley campus. But once he was inaugurated, the fuller implementation of decentralization through the remainder of the Sproul administration was inevitable. It is perhaps ironic that the inauguration of Franklin Murphy as chancellor at UCLA in 1960 carried with it the same imperative with regard to the more thorough decentralization undertaken during the latter period of the Kerr administration.

The title itself deserves some comment. Lee reports that there was substantial discussion among the regents and others with regard to the title. Several options appear to have been seriously considered. The first would be to continue to use provost as the title of the chief campus officer at Berkeley and Los Angeles. The second would have titled those officers president and used chancellor for the system head. The third was the one chosen.

These may appear to be distinctions without substance. I believe, however, that the symbolism in the naming decision was very significant. To continue the use of provost would have, in my opinion, led to a change of authority in degree rather than in kind. On the other hand, the capture of the title president for the campuses with chancellor being shifted to the central university position would have been perceived, as Sproul suggested, as "kicking the President upstairs." I believe that would likely have led to a looser confederation than was desirable or possible at that time.

The choice of chancellor as the title for the chief campus executive leaving the presidency as the office responsible for the University as a whole, was well designed to continue the one-university concept while initiating the process of placing real authority in the hands of an executive who could manage and lead the campuses in their pursuit of individual excellence.

I offer one further comment with regard to the title itself that comes out of more than a quarter-century of falling under its mantle, and through discussion with others who have carried the sobriquet chancellor. For some reason, it is a title that adheres to its holder in ways very different from any of the possible alternatives, e.g., provost or president. Not only is it almost universal to refer to the principal as Chancellor Young, but as The Chancellor or Mr. Chancellor or even simply Chancellor. This indicates an aura in connection with the term that is translatable into perceived prestige and authority which, if properly used, can be an added help in achieving appropriate institutional goals. Whether intended by those responsible for the title decision, in this sense as well, the choice was a good one.

So much for personal musings about the authority and prestige of the position that I have been privileged to hold for so many years. It and the campuses that the chancellors represent have changed substantially over the years since the process described in this excellent history was completed. They have changed not only in qualitative and quantitative terms, but especially in their complexity individually and in relation to the Office of the President, the regents, and the several publics that they serve. Since 1966 there have continued to be changes in degree in the administrative and governance interrelationships of these interdependent entities, but they have moved along the path that was set during the more than 20-year reorganization process kicked off by the PAS Study.

Only the first part of that process is described by Eugene Lee in this current work The rest, as Lee suggests, is "another story waiting to be told." It should be told.

Charles E. Young
Chancellor, UCLA

Eugene C. Lee

NOTES

Minutes of the Board of Regents are located in the Office of the Secretary of the Regents in Oakland, California. All other materials referenced below, excluding note 5, are located in the Bancroft Library at the University of California, Berkeley. (CU-5 refers to "Records of the President.")

1. Minutes of the Board of Regents, October 24, 1947.
2. Public Administration Service, *Report on Administrative Survey of the University of California*, (Chicago: Public Administration Service, 1948) (PAS *Report*).
3. J. Rafter to Miss Miller, December 26, 1950. University Archives, CU-5:1950:54.
4. James H. Corley to A. Alan Post, June 27, 1951. University Archives, CU-5:1951:54.
5. For a discussion of the governance of multicampus universities, including the University of California, see Eugene C. Lee and Frank M. Bowen, *The Multicampus University* (New York: McGraw-Hill Book Company, 1971), 481 pp.
6. PAS *Report*, 56.
7. Verne A. Stadtman, *The University of California 1868-1968* (New York: McGraw-Hill Book Company, 1970,) 257-58.
8. Stadtman, 272.
9. Minutes of the Board of Regents Committee on Educational Policy, December 13, 1935.
10. Stadtman, 272-73.
11. Stadtman, 272.
12. Memorandum to the Board of Regents Committee on Educational Policy, February 3, 1937. University Archives, CU-5: Box 1163, Administrative Reorganization I.
13. Stadtman, 273-74.
14. Minutes of the Board of Regents, June 12, 1942.
15. Stadtman notes that "the enumeration of the University's campuses varies at different points in history because of changes in concepts" (*op. cit.*, 569). In 1945, Hildebrand was probably referring to Mt. Hamilton and the Scripps Institution of Oceanography as "campuses," along with Berkeley, Davis, Los Angeles, San Francisco, and Santa Barbara.
16. Minutes of the Academic Senate, Northern Section, April 5, 1943, Vol. V, series II, 202.

17. Robert G. Sproul to George D. Louderback, April 21, 1943. (In Louderback, "Correspondence and Papers": letter in Box 11, folder on "Presidents 1938-1943").

18. Robert Gordon Sproul to files. University Archives, CU-5: Box 1163.

19. Plan of Administrative Organization—University of California, by Robert G. Sproul, originally enclosed with his letter to George D. Louderback, April 21, 1943 (in Louderback, "Correspondence and Papers," Carton 6, folder on "special committee on Organization, Misc. Drafts, Notes, etc.)."

20. Robert S. Johnson "A View from the Athletics and Administrative Side," an oral history conducted in 1984 by Suzanne B. Riess, in *Robert Gordon Sproul Oral History Project*, Regional Oral History Office, The Bancroft Library, University of California, Berkeley, 1986, 421-22.

21. George D. Louderback and Robert W. Hodgson, chairmen, respectively, of the northern and southern section special committees of the Academic Senate on University organization, October 23, 1943. University Archives, CU-5: Box 1163.

22. Undated and unsigned note in Louderback, "Correspondence and Papers," Box 11, folder on "Presidents 1938-1943".

23. "Resolution Adopted by Blue Shield," May 4, 1943. University Archives, CU-5: Administrative Reorganization III.

24. Excerpt from "Organization and Administrative Relations and Procedures: University of California at L.A.," August 10, 1943. University Archives, CU-5: Box 1163.

25. Minutes of the Board of Regents, October 22, 1943.

26. Robert G. Sproul to Clarence A. Dykstra, October 3, 1944 (in Minutes of the Board of Regents, October 27, 1944).

27. "Report of the Special Committee on Organization of the University, Academic Senate—Southern Section (revised May, 1944)." University Archives, CU-5: Box 1163.

28. "Report of the Special Committee on Organization (Northern Section Academic Senate) on Delegation of Administrative Functions," December 29, 1944. University Archives, CU-5: Box 1163.

29. Robert W. Hodgson to Robert G. Sproul, February 18, 1946. University Archives, CU-5: Box 1163.

30. *Faculty Bulletin*, March 8, 1946 (emphasis added).

31. Robert G. Sproul to Robert W. Hodgson, March 8, 1946. University Archives, CU-5: Box 1163.

32. Quoted in full in PAS, *Report*, 56-57.

33. Robert G. Sproul to Chairmen of Departments and Other Administrative Officers, November 14, 1946. University Archives, CU-5:1947:43.

34. Johnson, oral history, 421.

35. Minutes of the Board of Regents, January 24, 1947.

36. Cited in a letter from H. B. Walker, chairman to the Statewide University Committee, July 1, 1948. University Archives, CU-5:1948:680, July-September, folder 3 of 4.

37. Memorandum from the Committee on Simplification of University Procedure (Edwin A. Lee, chairman) to Robert G. Sproul, June 21, 1946. University Archives, CU-5:1948:17.

38. Russell Barthell and James H. Corley to Robert G. Sproul, October 9, 1947. University Archives, CU-5:1947:17.

39. Robert G. Sproul to James H. Corley, October 24, 1947. University Archives, CU-5:1947:17.

40. Minutes of the Board of Regents Committee on Finance and Business Management, October 24, 1947.

41. Clarence A. Dykstra, "Suggestions for Study by Public Administration Service," January 23, 1948. University Archives, CU-5:1948:17.

42. Letter to the author, May 8, 1992.

43. Memorandum from the Senate Advisory Committee to Public Administration Service, June 1, 1948. University Archives, CU-5: Box 1163, Administrative Organization IIA.

44. Robert G. Sproul to Herbert Olson, April 12, 1948. University Archives, CU-5: Box 1107:19a.

45. James H. Corley to Herbert Olson, April 12, 1948. University Archives, CU-5:1948:17.

46. Robert Rogers, "UCLA's Accounting Officer," an oral interview conducted in 1982 by James V. Mink, Oral History Program of The University Library, University of California at Los Angeles, 1987, 25, (emphasis added).

47. Johnson, oral history, 422.

48. PAS, *Report*, i.

49. *Ibid.*, ii.

50. *Ibid.*, 15-16.

51. *Ibid.*, 16.

52. *Ibid.*, 17.

53. *Ibid.*, 20-21, 33.
54. *Ibid.*, 23.
55. *Ibid.*, 24-25.
56. *Ibid.*, 25.
57. *Ibid.*, 30.
58. *Ibid.*, 57-59.
59. *Ibid.*, 72-73.
60. *Ibid.*, 79.
61. *Ibid.*, 79, 83.
62. *Ibid.*, 92-93.
63. *Ibid.*, 84.
64. *Ibid.*, 93.
65. *Ibid.*, 94.
66. *Ibid.*, 95.
67. *Ibid.*, 95-103.
68. *Ibid.*, 109.
69. *Ibid.*, 111.
70. Personal interview with Robert S. Johnson, September 10, 1991.
71. Baldwin Woods to Robert G. Sproul, May 19, 1948. University Archives, CU-5: Box 1107:19a.
72. Hugh Miller to Robert G. Sproul, September 24, 1948. University Archives, CU-5:1948:17.
73. Joel Hildebrand to Robert G. Sproul, September 23, 1948. University Archives, CU-5:1948:54.
74. Robert G. Sproul to Deans, September 1, 1948. University Archives, CU-5: Box 1163.
75. James H. Corley to Robert G. Sproul, October 4, 1948. University Archives, CU-5:1948:17.
76. Claude B. Hutchinson to Robert G. Sproul, September 21, 1948. University Archives, CU-5:1948:17.
77. Clarence A. Dykstra to Robert G. Sproul, September 8, 1948. University Archives, CU-5:1948:17.
78. Letter with enclosure from A. R. Davis to Robert G. Sproul, September 28, 1948. University Archives, CU-5: Box 1163, Administrative Organization IIA.
79. Malcolm M. Davisson to Robert G. Sproul, September 23, 1948. University Archives, CU-5:1948:17.
80. O. Lundberg to Robert G. Sproul, June 30, 1948. University Archives, CU-5: Box 1107:19a.

81. Letter from Knowles Ryerson to Robert G. Sproul, August 7, 1948; letter from Sproul to Ryerson, August 17, 1948. University Archives, CU-5:1948:680 July-September, folder 3 of 4.

82. Knowles Ryerson to Robert G. Sproul, September 7, 1948. University Archives, CU-5:1948:17.

83. Dykstra to Sproul, September 28, 1948.

84. James A. C. Grant, "Comparative Constitutional Law at UCLA," an oral interview conducted by Steven J. Novak, Oral History Program of the University Library, University of California at Los Angeles, 1989, 142.

85. Hansena Frederickson, "UCLA Administration, 1936-1966," an oral interview conducted in 1966 by James V. Mink, Oral History Program, Department of Special Collections, The University Library, University of California at Los Angeles, 1969, 42-43.

86. Paul A. Dodd, "Patient Persuaders," an oral interview conducted in 1981 by Thomas Bertonneau, Oral History Program, Department of Special Collections, The University Library, University of California at Los Angeles, 1985, 280.

87. Andrew J. Hamilton, "UCLA Public Affairs Officer," an oral interview conducted in 1966 by James V. Mink, Oral History Program, Department of Special Collections, The University Library, University of California at Los Angeles, 1972, 74.

88. Ryerson to Sproul, August 17, 1948.

89. Dykstra to Sproul, September 28, 1948.

90. Corley to Sproul, October 4, 1948.

91. James H. Corley, "Serving the University in Sacramento," an oral interview conducted in 1967 by Verne A. Stadtman, Regional Oral History Office, The Bancroft Library, University of California, Berkeley, 1969, 100-01.

92. O. Lundberg to Robert G. Sproul, July 12, 1948. University Archives, CU-5: Box 1107:19a.

93. Herman A. Spindt to Robert G. Sproul, September 10, 1948. University Archives, CU-5:1948:17.

94. Hutchinson to Sproul, September 21, 1948.

95. Report to Sproul of the Committee to study expansion of University facilities (H. B. Walker, chairman). University Archives, CU-5:1948-680, July-September, folder 3 of 4.

96. Edward S. Rogers, M.D. to Robert G. Sproul, September 4, 1948. University Archives, CU-5: Box 1211a, Administrative Reorganization IX.

97. Robert Webb to Sproul, September 9, 1948. University Archives, CU-5: 1948:17.

98. Minutes of the President's Administrative Advisory Conference, March 30, 1949. University Archives, CU-5: Box 1163.

99. See David P. Gardner, *The California Oath Controversy*, Berkeley, University of California Press, 1967.

100. Charles C. Teague to Robert G. Sproul, April 27, 1949. University Archives, CU-5:1949:54.

101. Robert Gordon Sproul to Robert Underhill, July 6, 1949. University Archives, CU-5:1949:54.

102. Minutes of the Special Committee, February 9, 1950. University Archives, CU-5: Administrative Reorganization II.

103. *Ibid.*

104. Minutes of the Board of Regents Special Committee to consider the Report of the Public Administration Service, June 10 and September 16, 1949. University Archives, CU-4ar: Regents Special Committee on Administrative Reorganization, June 10, 1949 to March 30, 1951. Minutes of the Board of Regents, September 23, 1949 and February 24, 1950.

105. Johnson, oral history, 420-21.

106. Gardner, 7-8.

107. Minutes of the Board of Regents, September 23, 1949 and February 24, 1950.

108. Minutes of the Special Committee, February 9, 1950. University Archives, CU-5: Administrative Reorganization II.

109. Robert G. Sproul to George Adams, November 7, 1949. University Archives, CU-5:1949:54.

110. Report of a Subcommittee on Appointment of a Provost at UCLA to the Board of Regents Committee on Southern California Schools, Colleges, and Institutions, October 11, 1950. University Archives, CU-4ar: Regents Special Committee.

111. Robert G. Sproul to the Committee on Southern California Schools, Colleges and Institutions, October 26, 1950. University Archives, CU-5: Administrative Reorganization II.

112. *Ibid.*

113. Transcript of the joint meeting of the Regents' Special Committee on Administrative Reorganization and the Committee on Southern California Schools, Colleges, and Institutions, December 13, 1950. University Archives, CU-5: Box 1163.

114. Minutes of a joint meeting of the Committee on Southern California Schools, Colleges, and Institutions and the Special Committee on Administrative Reorganization, February 9, 1951. University Archives, CU-5: Administrative Reorganization II.

115. *Ibid.*

116. Minutes of a joint meeting of the Committee on Southern California Schools, Colleges, and Institutions and the Special Committee on Administrative Reorganization, December 13, 1950. University Archives CU-5: Administrative Reorganization II.

117. University of California, *Faculty Bulletin*, April 1951.

118. Minutes of the Board of Regents, January 25, 1952.

119. *Ibid.*

120. T. R. McConnell, T. C. Holy, and H. H. Semans, "A Restudy of the Needs of California in Higher Education," (Sacramento: State Department of Education, 1955).

121. *Ibid.*, 224-27.

122. *Ibid.*, 230-31.

123. *Ibid.*, 231.

124. *Ibid.*, 232-34.

125. Johnson, oral history, 422-23.

126. For a brief summary of administrative reorganization during the administration of Clark Kerr, see "Development and Decentralization: The Administration of the University of California, 1958-1966," a report of the Office of the President issued in 1966.